Praise for *Forest +*

"Reading *Forest + Home* feels like taking a ..... the woods with your warmest and witchi..... reverence for and curiosity about the natural world are evident in every page of this jewel of a book, and they're contagious too—I will never look at the world around me with anything less than absolute wonder ever again."

— CARA NICOLETTI, founder of Seemore Meats & Veggies

+ + +

"Beautifully intertwined with storytelling and nostalgia, *Forest + Home* is an intimate collection of cookery and herbalism, an approach that feels both accessible and celebratory. It is almost certain to become a dog-eared classic, frequently revisited throughout the seasons."

— ANJA ROTHE, owner of Fat of the Land

+ + +

"*Forest + Home* is a taste of the wild for a modern palate. Each recipe is a perfect mashup of foraged finds and grocery store ingredients. Whether you're a seasoned or a fledgling forager you'll find your way easily with Spencre's recipes and advice for making a delectable meal. A cookbook for the adventurous!"

— CHERYL RAFUSE, Owner + Head Gardener at Plant Magic Gardens

Forest
+Home

Disclaimer

The recipes and information in this book are meant to inspire. This content is not meant to diagnose or treat any ailment. Please consult a physician or clinical herbalist before beginning any new herbal routine.

When foraging for herbs, please consult a professional before consumption. This cookbook is not a foraging guidebook and cannot be held responsible for any mistakes made in the wild.

Forest +Home

Cultivating an Herbal Kitchen

Foreword by
Hilarie Burton Morgan

Spencre McGowan

Andrews McMeel
PUBLISHING®

To Connor,
for everything.
I goat you.

Foreword

Do you remember that feeling in adolescence when you were old enough to have a small level of independence but still maintain the largeness of your imagination? Do you remember those rambles in the woods and the forts and those walks after dark that felt deliciously rebellious? The feeling that woodland spirits were real and perhaps watching you? The feeling of possibility?

I crave that sense memory. I search for it in places I travel to and in songs on the radio and in clothes I pull down from the attic. And when you find that memory, you want to hug it close and live in it for a while. I had a similar sense memory the very first time I saw Spencre's book *Blotto Botany*.

I'd ventured to Salem, Massachusetts, for the very first time with my children in tow. It was a pilgrimage under a full harvest moon in mid-October, and I wanted them to have an epic, magical experience. They did. And I, fortunately, got to see it all through their eyes. It had been such a dreamy trip that I'd wanted a souvenir to capture that tingly feeling so I could carry it back to our farm and keep it for a lifetime. The kitschy gift shops with Christmas ornaments and mass-produced knickknacks didn't jump out to me. I'd been told about HausWitch Home + Healing, the most perfect shop in the most perfect historic corner-store space, with thoughtfully sourced tools and comforts for witches and wanderers alike. And so, as we wrapped up our trip, we landed there.

What was it about that tiny green book that captivated me? I can't remember looking at anything else, really. I picked it up and knew it had been written just for me—a collection of potions and practices to take back to the farm and study over the long winter months ahead. Spencre's handwritten style reminded me of notes passed in between classes, journals shared back and forth with a bosom friend. Her sense of curiosity and enthusiasm to share her discoveries felt empowering. If she could do it, we all could.

As happens now, we began a correspondence that spanned thousands of miles but that felt as easy as a neighborly chat over a chain-link fence. And that is Spencre's way. She forges ahead and locates the magic—as one would morels or a tangle of ripe berries—and then she doubles back to share the excitement with the rest of us.

Forest + Home is a testament to her creativity and her unique ability to recall the sense memory of food. As much as old concert T-shirts and the smell of ocean air take us back to golden hours of the past, food is a sense memory that Spencre uses to combine affection and awareness of our environment and appreciation for the tiny treasures of daily life.

I have already dog-eared multiple recipes in this book and will pair them with the fruit shrubs I learned to make from Spencre's last book. It is a powerful gift to have friends you can learn from, and I feel so fortunate to have crossed forest trails with this magical little witch.

Xoxo
Hilarie Burton Morgan

Introduction

The first dinner party I ever hosted was a disaster. I was sixteen, my dad was out of town, and my friend Tasha and I decided to invite a few people over for a cozy little meal. Not having much money, or any know-how of cooking more than a box of mac 'n' cheese, we boiled a bunch of spaghetti and threw the ball of mozzarella we found in the fridge directly in the pot with the water. After straining the rubbery mess, we garnished the dish with a sprinkle of cheese and cold blueberries. I remember sitting on the floor in silence while my friends ate their meals, knowing that everyone was thinking the same thing I was: "What a horrid mess." To this day, I cringe over the meal, but my friends still try to convince me that it wasn't that bad, but I'm trying to make up for it to this day.

I never expected to become a cook. After being raised in commercial kitchens around New England, thanks to my chef dad, it wasn't the sort of stress I wanted to deal with, and making food didn't interest me much at first. When I moved to California to attend herb school, I fully intended on becoming a midwife once it was done. I studied, trained as a doula, and toured a school for midwifery in Maine, but my path kept wandering back to the kitchen. In 2016, I started making recipe zines and selling them on my new herbal cooking blog, *Gingertooth & Twine*. I told everyone around me that I didn't want to be making food and recipes for others to use, but I felt I had to do something "big" with my herbalist training. What I didn't realize at the time was that cooking was the thing that was bringing me the most joy. I was obsessed with finding new ways to incorporate herbs into my meals. I devoured cookbooks by day and spent all my time at a library in Maine, trying to find my recipe style while experimenting with different ways to make the perfect herby latte or loaf of bread.

Food influences all of us, whether or not we realize it. It sustains us, frustrates us, gives us something to talk about, and allows us to experience the world in our own way. *Forest + Home* is a celebration of the life we live alongside our meals. The name is an ode to my exploration of food through my love of the forest, nature, and the many homes I've had over the years. To me, there isn't much of a divide between the experience we have in nature and in our home. We bring flowers and trees into our safe places to make them feel more natural. We cook with plants that have been ground up, dried, and sold in plastic. We live in houses made of broken-down trees. If we are readily adding pieces of our natural experience to our homes, why not go one step further by adding medicinal plants in our everyday cooking?

My goal is to bring the aspects of the healing outdoor world into your home, no matter where you live. Even if you have to bring a butane stove onto your fire escape and toss a handful of rose petals into what you're cooking, I can guarantee you will have a memorable experience; you'll feel satisfied with your endeavor. Cooking and healing are similar in the respect that both are lifelong journeys, and both will entail many mistakes made along the way. I can't tell you how many times I've messed up and cried over a nettle dumpling (I'm still trying to figure it out) or experienced anxiety about what I "should" be doing to heal rather than what I can. After thirty-two years in this world, the only thing I can tell you for sure is that the forest can lift your mood and so can a damn fine plate of pasta. My ideal world is where the two are combined in a respectful and exciting way, and I can't wait to share them both with you.

Herbal Practices

Every culture has a history of working with medicinal herbs. Some of that history is recorded; some is passed down through action and storytelling. There are methods that can be learned from all sorts of ancient herbal practices, but digging deeper into your own ancestral wisdom is powerful and healing in its own right. For example, my lineage lies in Scandinavia and Ireland, so I root my practice in herbs from those regions. I consume nettles and elderflowers and find solace in the plants that are native to my ancestors' lands. I have developed a keen sense of respect for plants and do my best to appreciate, not appropriate, the ones that are not native to my bloodline. Knowing my ancestral lineage and being able to trace the plants they traditionally used is a privilege that is not lost on me.

I tell you, sweet reader, all of this in hopes that you, too, will learn the value of your own ancestral plants if you are able and educate yourself on the history, growing habits, and traditional practice of the plants that grow around you. Stay educated on the Indigenous people who reside on the land you live on and came before you. By doing this, I fully believe that the respect you hold for any plant will be transferred back to you with good health. This may sound out there, but at herb school, we were taught the spiritual practices of plants right alongside the scientific practices. And this is something that I carry with me to this day, from when I teach a class to when I harvest a nettle plant—every plant has a story to tell. My hope is that you'll learn how to be open to hearing each story.

Why Cook with Herbs?

Why I cook with herbs is something I often think about. But when it comes down to it, we, as humans, cook more than we do anything else. Our lives revolve around food, whether that be a hard-headed diet, a casual dinner at home, or a drunken night involving delivery. So when we cook, why not make it herbal?

Cooking with medicinal herbs is my number one way to introduce healing plants into my body. Not only is it the easiest way but also the herbs have the greatest impact when they're in food. Seldom are the days when I make daily teas or consciously consume tinctures for healing. While I'd like to remain in that realm of medicinal practice, in reality, cooking with nourishing plants has become my primary source of herbal intake.

When we cook with herbs, I believe that we are cooking with the basic tools and spices we were given by nature. Our common culinary spices and herbs are popular for a reason. We love basil for its bright, flavorful energy, but how often do we take notice of the medicinal values behind it? Have you considered the impact of adding some lemon balm or stinging nettles to your food? Not only is cooking with herbs a fantastic way to add nutrients but also it's a simple way to learn the basics of herbalism.

So will adding a spoonful of lemon balm to some dough immediately heal all your ailments? Absolutely not. But that isn't how medicine (of any sort) works. Sure, some things are instantaneous, but medicine, especially herbal, is typically a practice of routine. Healing isn't a quick, straight, and narrow path to feeling better. You learn the art of healing over time by adding herbs to your food. The more you know about a plant's flavor and texture, the easier it will be to add it to your food. In the Nettle Pasta recipe (page 163), the nettle has been completely broken down from the plant before the harvest. It's been dried, crushed, then powdered so fine that it essentially becomes flour. In the herbal simple syrups on page 84, the plant is essentially transformed into a liquid that can be used for anything, from making a fun cocktail to brushing it on a cake. The many ways of incorporating medicinal herbs into your food are endless. My goal with this book is to give you the simplest tools to carry with you as you learn and grow on your own herbal path. Creativity and fearlessness in the kitchen are when your healing journey begins.

How to Use This Book

This book is organized seasonally and broken down in the way I find the most useful for herbal cooking. You'll find information on my herbal practices and my favorite herbs to cook with. I kept it pretty simple, and you'll notice that the amount of herbs needed to keep in your herbal kitchen pantry is not overly extravagant. I like to boil everything down to five or so herbs that I keep on hand and know inside and out. If the only thing you take away from this book is how to infuse nettle or dandelion leaves into your food, then I consider my job done. My hope is that you can use this book as a guide for trusting your instincts, playing with ingredients, using good salt, and, most importantly, having fun in the kitchen.

Herbalism is not meant to be overwhelming or intimidating. While the work of a clinical herbalist (someone who prescribes specific remedies to clients) is complicated and strategic, the work of a kitchen witch is intuitive, thoughtful, and full of flavor. Take one herb at a time. Learn how it tastes, discern its uses and contradictions, and discover how you like to cook with it. I always advise people to get to know a plant like you would get to know a lover or a new friend. Take your time to navigate the intricate ways that each individual herb works for your own body. We've all got the capability to heal and make good food. Just remember to not overthink it too much.

Medicinal Kitchen Herbs

These are the herbs that I like to keep in the kitchen for easy use while cooking. I put them in a mix of jars and keep them within arm's reach of the stove. Different from the common spice rack herbs, these plants are more traditionally used in herbal medicine. However, for the sake of your new herbal cooking adventure, they, too, will become staples in your kitchen! You can find a glossary for terms of herbal actions on page 198. Herbal actions are used to identify the primary use of a medicinal herb. They are terms specific to the healing properties of a plant.

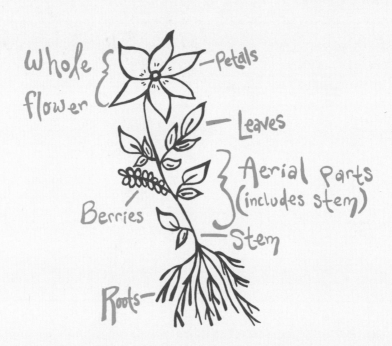

Ashwagandha *(Withania somnifera)*

> **Parts used:** Root
>
> **Actions:** Adaptogen, nervine, anti-inflammatory, tonic, aphrodisiac
>
> **Taste:** Bitter, earthy, pungent

Native to India, ashwagandha is a widely used plant in Ayurvedic medicine. It roughly translates to "smell of a horse." It's an adaptogenic and a nervine, known for its use in calming the nervous system, combating stress, and aiding sleep. It is also said to help cerebral function. Its use as an anti-inflammatory makes it good medicine for joint and nerve pain. The powder makes a great addition to food and smoothies. However, be wary of adding too much at one time—the taste can be overpowering. From my own experience, ashwagandha can get bitter really fast. I wouldn't advise adding over 1 tablespoon of the powdered root at a time.

Burdock *(Arctium)*

> **Parts used:** Root and seeds
>
> **Actions:** Bitter, diuretic, alterative, hepatic
>
> **Taste:** Bitter, earthy

Burdock is one of those medicinal plants that can be eaten like a vegetable. The root resembles a smaller, darker carrot or parsnip and tastes great when roasted or added to soups. Burdock is known for helping with skin conditions such as eczema or psoriasis, with long-term use. It also works as a bitter, helping bile production and making digestion easier.

Calendula *(Calendula officinalis)*

> **Parts used:** Flowers
>
> **Actions:** Lymphatic, alterative, antispasmodic, diaphoretic, astringent
>
> **Taste:** Mild, floral

Calendula is a very lovely, mild herb to incorporate into your kitchen habits. Sometimes called pot marigold, calendula can be identified by its bright open petals that resemble that of a daisy. Calendula can be used topically to treat a number of skin conditions, burns, and stings and as a natural dye for fabric (it makes a beautiful golden color). Internally, calendula is fantastic for stimulating the lymphatic system and aiding the digestive system. Its mild taste makes it the perfect addition to food. Add it to compound butter (page 96), medicinal broths (page 175), pasta, salads, etc.

Chamomile *(Matricaria chamomilla)*

> **Parts used:** Flowers
>
> **Actions:** Nervine, tonic, antispasmodic, astringent, carminative
>
> **Taste:** Bitter, sweet, honey, apple

It's safe to say that chamomile is a well-known and widely used herb. Look at any tea intended for sleep and you'll most likely find chamomile on the ingredient list. While tea is great, chamomile makes a lovely addition to food, especially baked goods. As a nervine, it soothes nerves and can

ffee double strength. Heat
lk to scalding. Pour hot
e amounts at same time,
nger than usual. Use 3 to 4
Serve in small cups.
lasse with whipped cream.
ffee as usual, but use
Pour over crushed ice.

butter, 2 eggs and milk fro
Put spoonful of instant eg
dd milk and sugar. Put
add 2 cups hot water f
should be boiling no
up and cover eggs wi
on under eggs and butt
et timer for eggs, relax
rain, forget it; try aga
pati 1962.

Bonne Maman
an-Yuzu Spread
Wt 1oz (28g⊖)

doors closed & doors opening (ou).

m flower & leaf, marshmallow
wood betony .)(o o o o o o o o .

TURMERIC

Kerr

Eld

calm the mind. It also works wonders for digestive issues, such as indigestion or an upset stomach. Though the flavor can be bitter, chamomile is great when paired with a savory dish or when made into a syrup (see the Rose Simple Syrup recipe on page 84). Use fresh flowers on top of cakes or salads for extra medicinal oomph.

Dandelion *(Taraxacum officinale)*

> **Parts used:** Flowers, leaves, root
> **Actions:** Tonic, diuretic, bitter, nutrient, mild laxative
> **Taste:** Bitter, floral

Dandelion is a powerhouse of a plant. Branded as an obnoxious weed, dandelion is anything but. A powerful digestive aid, this flower provides a wealth of health benefits and makes an incredible addition to your cooking routine. Its bitter quality is a major attribute of the dandelion, as bitter herbs increase bile production in the gallbladder and enhance the digestive process. The root, when roasted, makes a fantastic coffee substitute, and the leaves can be used in place of almost any typical culinary green. The yellow flower can be used to make syrups or fried up as hushpuppies (page 56). When using the flower, make sure to remove all green bits to reduce bitterness. Only harvest dandelions from spaces you know have not been sprayed with weed killer or affected by dog or human waste. Avoid harvesting from the sides of trails and public parks.

Elder *(Sambucus)*

> **Parts used:** Flower and berry
> **Actions:** Diaphoretic, antispasmodic, antirheumatic, expectorant
> **Taste:** Floral, fruity (almost pear- or apple-like)

Elderflower . . . I need little else but the memory of taste to be transported back to so many herbal culinary memories with this flower. Sprinkled on any baked good or made into a beautiful cordial, elderflower is bound to bring a smile to anyone's face. Elderflower is helpful when dealing with colds and flu and can reduce swollen sinuses.

The berries are also excellent flavor-wise, but they must be processed with heat to avoid any potential toxins. Often, you'll find elderberry syrup used for cold and flu care, but you may luck out and find a jar of elderberry jam at your local farmers' market.

Ginger *(Zingiber officinale)*

> **Parts used:** Root
> **Actions:** Carminative, emmenagogue, anti-inflammatory, diaphoretic
> **Taste:** Spicy, sweet, pungent, peppery

Ginger is a culinary ingredient that often is not acknowledged for its medicinal benefits. While spicy and pungent, ginger is a wonderful plant known for its carminative (aka digestive) power. Ginger is said to soothe nausea, inflammation, and stomach aches, as well as being a lovely additive to baking and savory dishes. Powdered, minced, or pureed, ginger can be used in a variety of ways.

Lavender *(Lavandula officinalis)*

    Parts used: Flowers

    Actions: Nervine, carminative, aromatic, analgesic, vulnerary, antifungal

    Taste: Floral, earthy, bitter if overdone

Lavender is another one of those herbs that many of us grew up with in some form. I love adding a bit of dried lavender to anything from Lavender Macaroons (page 184) to Lavender-Matcha Iced Lattes (page 64) or even just keeping a small cotton bag of it under my pillow for a good night's rest. Lavender is a nervine, which means that it helps the body restore and calm your nerves. It's a highly aromatic herb, and the smell is distinct and easily recognizable. It can also be helpful for settling an upset stomach, easing headaches, and reducing anxiety.

Lemon Balm *(Melissa officinalis)*

    Parts used: Leaves

    Actions: Aromatic, adaptogen, nervine, antispasmodic, carminative

    Taste: Citrusy, bright, minty, floral

Herbalist Nicholas Culpeper once said that lemon balm "causeth the mind and heart to become merry." Not only is it one of my favorite herbs to cook with (I'll basically add it to anything) but also it's one of my go-to herbs when I need to calm down, relieve anxiety, or soothe an upset stomach. It's flavorful, cheerful, and wildly easy to grow in a garden. I keep a jar of dried lemon balm within arm's reach at all times.

Maca *(Lepidium meyenii)*

    Parts used: Root

    Actions: Adaptogen, aphrodisiac

    Taste: Bitter, nutty

Also known as Peruvian ginseng, maca is known for promoting a healthy immune system and physical endurance. Maca can be very energizing, so it's best to take it in the morning. As an adaptogen, it can also be used to help your body cope with feelings of stress and anxiety. Maca has a lovely warm, nutty flavor that is easily hidden when added to food.

Matcha *(Camellia sinensis)*

    Taste: Grassy, sweet

While not technically considered a medicinal herb, matcha is widely known for its health benefits. Matcha means "finely powdered tea" and is made from the young leaves of the tea plant. You'll recognize matcha from its bold green color and grassy flavor. This grassy flavor is easily transformed into a wonderful, sweet flavor when added to baked goods. Matcha is used in traditional Japanese tea ceremonies and is native to Asia.

Nettles *(Uritca diotica)*

    Parts used: Leaves and root

    Actions: Diuretic, astringent, tonic

    Taste: Earthy, creamy

Also known as stinging nettles, nettles are my number one go-to for herbal cooking. They are considered one of the most applicable herbs and have a wide range of uses. Not to mention they are one of the easiest herbs to identify. Herbalist Nicholas Culpeper once said, "They may be found by feeling for them in the darkest night." You may in fact be familiar with the sting of the nettle, which often strikes people with fear surrounding using it in the kitchen. But the nettle works its magic both internally and externally. It's used as an aid for skin conditions such as eczema, and it processes high yields of chlorophyll, vitamin C, and fiber. My former teacher David Hoffman famously said, "When in doubt, use nettles." This is a great testament to the versatility of this wonderful plant.

Try to avoid harvesting nettles that have already gone to seed, as they not only are tough to eat but also can also interfere with kidney function because the older plant produces cystoliths, aka deposits of calcium carbonate. This is why I like to harvest them as soon as they pop up in Montana, then blanch and freeze them for later use. You can learn how to do this on page 39.

Reishi *(Ganoderma lucidum)*

    Parts used: Fruiting body

    Actions: Anti-inflammatory, tonic, adaptogen

    Taste: Mushroom, bitter, chocolate

Reishi and I have had a long love affair with each other. It's a mushroom that I keep on hand (both sliced and powdered) at all times. Also known as the "mushroom of immortality," it has been used for thousands of years in Chinese medicine to support the immune system, help the body adapt to stress, and provide some mental clarity. I like to add some dried slices of reishi to soups and broths or make a syrup with it. The powder is an excellent addition to desserts that include chocolate or coffee, as the flavors really complement each other. Check out the No-Bake Peanut Butter–Reishi Cookies (page 149). Keep in mind that reishi needs heat to properly extract its medicinal benefits.

Rose *(Rosa spp.)*

    Parts used: Petals and whole flower

    Actions: Aromatic, nervine, aphrodisiac, antispasmodic, emmenagogue, uterine tonic

    Taste: Floral, sweet, astringent if overdone

Oh, the beloved rose. Known by many all over the world, the rose is wonderful for emotional turmoil and matters of the heart. Rose is considered a gentle antispasmodic and a uterine tonic (make a cup of rose tea for menstrual cramps). When using rose petals, make sure to use food-grade rose petals. Most store-bought petals are sprayed with preservatives and are not intended for consumption. The beach rose (*Rosa rugosa*) is ideal for wildcrafting and medicine making.

Rosehips *(Rosa canina)*

Parts used: Berry
Actions: Anti-inflammatory
Taste: Fruity, bright, floral

Rosehips are an excellent source of vitamin C and have been used to treat illnesses such as colds, flus, and respiratory conditions for generations. Rosehips are considered an anti-inflammatory and can be helpful in treating the pain associated with arthritis. Rosehips are also excellent for the skin, considering how much vitamin C they contain.

Shatavari *(Asparagus racemosus)*

Parts used: Root
Actions: Adaptogen
Taste: Bitter, nutty, sweet

The name means "woman with a hundred husbands," which speaks to the power it has on the reproductive system. Shatavari is related to the common asparagus plant and has a wide range of benefits for everyone, from fighting inflammation to coping with stress and even aiding respiratory health. The plant contains phytoestrogens, which are plant-based compounds that mimic estrogen, making it an ideal herb for menopause. Shatavari root is often found in powdered form, which makes it ideal for infusing into foods, like the Shatavari Kale Caesar Salad (page 81).

Tulsi/Holy Basil *(Ocimum tenuiflorum)*

Parts used: Ariel parts
Actions: Adaptogenic, nervine, carminative, aromatic, demulcent
Taste: Floral, peppery, bright, earthy

For one of the first classes I taught, I made a syrup for a mocktail that was pretty heavy handed with tulsi. Erica, the owner of the shop, came up to me after class—her cheeks a cheery rose color and sporting a giddy look—and asked me whether I had put alcohol in the drink. I told her I hadn't, but I was feeling the same. I concluded that it was likely due to the tulsi in the syrup. Tulsi can work wonders for our emotional health, and it's another herb that I am very fond of adding to almost everything. The taste is florally, bright, and slightly peppery, making it great for savory dishes or mixing it into a homemade dough. Tulsi is widely used in Ayurvedic medicine and is considered a sacred plant, hence the name "holy basil." There are three different types of holy basil, all with slightly different taste profiles: Rama, Vana, and Krishna. The latter is the one I use most often because of its peppery flavor.

Turmeric *(Curcuma longa)*

> **Parts used:** Root
>
> **Actions:** Anti-inflammatory, antioxidant
>
> **Taste:** Earthy, sweet, pungent

Turmeric is an herb and spice that I think most people are aware of these days. It's been given the well-deserved reputation of helping with inflammation and joint pain relief above anything else. It's easy to take in capsule form but even easier to include in your food. To properly extract the medicinal benefits of turmeric, it's best combined with black pepper or a high-quality fat. Also, keep in mind that some people do have allergic reactions to turmeric, so it's not suitable for everyone.

Classic Culinary Herbs

Here is a simple overview of what everyday, more commonly known spices and culinary herbs can do for you.

Basil: An aromatic herb, basil aids in reducing anxiety and is considered to have anti-inflammatory benefits. Chew on a fresh leaf to neutralize bad breath.

Black Pepper: This is helpful with digestion and warming the intestines. Pepper is actually a dried berry from the *Piper nigrum* plant, and its aromatic and digestive properties are best maintained when the peppercorn is whole.

Cardamom: These little pods are full of medicinal benefits, including diuretic properties and those that aid digestive health. Cardamom is also known to help battle bad breath, so chew on that (pun intended) if you find yourself in need.

Cayenne: As a first aid method, you can sprinkle cayenne on a small kitchen cut to slow bleeding before seeking other treatment. I know this sounds counterintuitive, but it actually works and shouldn't sting ya!

Cinnamon: This is a warming spice that can help with circulation and add a lovely bit of heat to whatever you add it to. I like to add it to unexpected foods, such as the Pickled Onions (page 194).

Fennel: Oh, lovely fennel. . . . This is a fantastic herb for digestive health. You can use the seeds, root, or aerial parts in cooking. Fennel root processes a more mild fennel flavor than the seeds or even the green aerial parts of the plant. Try it in Dad's Quahog Chowder (page 150). Make a tea of the seeds when dealing with an upset stomach or bloat.

Garlic: We all know garlic as the pungent little bulb that adds a magnitude of flavor to our food. But did you also know that it's a very effective antimicrobial? Garlic aids the respiratory system and ailments such as bronchitis and influenza. It is also thought to support the good natural bacterial flora in the digestive system.

Rosemary: In many witchy texts, you will often find rosemary described as a memory aid. When I was seventeen, I sewed some rosemary into a cloth bracelet and wore it around my wrist all summer in hopes of improving my own memory. I actually don't remember whether it worked! Anyway, rosemary is a lovely aromatic herb and a staple in my kitchen. In addition to cooking with it, I like to dry a few sprigs on my windowsill and burn them to cover any bad smells in the house.

Sage: Sage is a wonderful culinary staple and can be made into a tea for congestion when dealing with colds and flus. I like pairing sage with rose petals when I'm feeling under the weather. Sage is a bitter, aromatic herb, so try a less-is-more approach when using it medicinally or while cooking. While there are many types of sage, I refer to culinary sage throughout this book.

Thyme: Thyme is a FANTASTIC lung tonic. It's definitely underutilized in this respect, but I've had wonderful success with drinking thyme as a tea for lung remedy. It is also considered an antifungal, so it could be helpful when dealing with mold in your home.

Edible Flowers

Violets

Calendula

Nasturtiums

Dandelion

Rose

Lavender

Red Clover

Borage

Butterfly Pea Flower

Cornflower

Never consume flowers that you aren't 100 percent sure haven't been sprayed with weed killer or preservatives. Unless specified for food use, many store-bought flowers are sprayed, so keep this in mind. And if in doubt, always ask!

Adaptogenic Herbs

Adaptogens are herbs that can help your body adapt to stress, increase vitality, and boost your immune system. I mention them frequently throughout this book since they are easily adaptable to cooking and, with their rising popularity, accessible and easy to find in stores these days. Adaptogenic powders come in many forms and are often mixed with other, more palatable herbs that make them perfect for consumption. Adaptogens are best when used daily and long term. Capsules are the easiest way to take them, but if you are the type to remember to add them to your daily meals, it's a fantastic way to get medicinal herbs into your routine.

Some of my favorite adaptogens to cook with are:

reishi mushroom

ashwagandha

shatavri

maca

You can find brief descriptions of these herbs on pages 5-10, but I also recommend the book *Adaptogens: Herbs for Strength, Stamina, and Stress Relief* by David Winston and Steven Maimes for further study.

Remember that not every adaptogen works for everyone. It's always best to consult a clinical herbalist or practitioner when incorporating new herbs into your daily routine.

Sourcing Herbs

The most common questions I get asked about herbalism are where to get herbs and what to look for when buying them. Luckily, bulk herbs seem to be quite easy to source these days, thanks to herbalism's rising popularity and, of course, the internet.

Where do I find my herbs, and how do I know whether they are of good quality?
Sourcing quality herbs is easier than you'd think. When I worked as the onsite herbalist for a small natural food store in Maine, I spent a lot of time on the phone with a major herb supplier. One of my main questions for them was, **What is the difference between organic herbs and nonorganic? And is there a significant difference in quality?**

The answer was while organic herbs are certified and documented as organic, most major herb companies spend a lot of time making sure that their herbs are grown well and with intention. These companies should, most often do, care about the quality and reputation of their herbs, so everything you see from them is going to be safe for consumption and free of pesticides. And they supply their workers with quality wages and working conditions. If you are questioning anything, please call a company's customer support line and voice whatever concerns you may have. A good company will be able to answer your questions without getting defensive.

Where do I find these herbs?
Many natural food stores have a bulk herb section, which is such a lifesaver. Google will be your bestie when finding herbs if you don't already have a designated spot. Type in your local natural food store and ask whether they carry the bulk herb you are looking for. If they don't have it, ask whether they can special order it for you. Most often, they will be able to do this. If you're lucky enough to have an actual herb shop nearby, they will most definitely be able to special order any herb you are looking for if they don't have it in stock. I have provided a list of trusted bulk herb companies that you can directly purchase from online (see page 99). Most natural food and herb shops buy wholesale from these companies.

But what if I want to buy locally?
Again, Google is going to be your best friend here. Search for local farms and feel free to call or email them to see whether they grow the herb that you are looking for. Also, scope out your local farmers' markets and talk directly to the growers to see what they offer. Oftentimes, farmers will have herbs that they don't always sell at the market or most likely will have an idea where you can find whatever herb you are looking for.

Find your local herbalist.
I've lived in many different types of places, from cities, to the middle of redwoods, to this tiny cabin I currently call home in Montana. There is bound to be an herbalist in your county who is willing to help you find what you are looking for. Herbalists are community-oriented people, so don't hesitate to reach out!!

Should You Buy Organic?

Short answer: Please do not worry about strictly buying organic if it's not in your budget.

Whenever I teach a class, I try to stress the importance of using what you have access to. In a perfect world, we'd dig up potatoes and cut chamomile from our very own gardens and find untouched fruits and veggies at our local stores. But this isn't that sort of world, and from where I am, this is America—where food deserts make up a good portion of our nation's lands and most of us work two or more jobs just to live paycheck to paycheck. Americans are obsessed with at-home health solutions. Many of us are even willing to dole out $70 on a powdered herbal supplement even if we can't really afford it. My goal as an herbalist is to not push that agenda onto you. I want you to feel good about the food you eat and get your herbs in any way you can. Herbalism was instilled by people for people, but it has fallen prey to capitalism and elitism, especially with the rise of social media and influencer culture.

When it comes to organic foods, I will, of course, advise you to go for it whenever possible. But my biggest fear is that you will get caught up in the pressure of what you *should* buy instead of what you *can* buy. Despite the privilege I've had of growing up near markets with a wide range of nourishing food options, I have succumbed to the purchases that were beyond my means just because I felt like I should be buying organic. My thought is that you should **buy what you can**.

Here are some tips I've picked up over the years:

+ Pay attention to the quality of your food, but don't get hung up on whether it has that organic sticker.

+ Scan the ingredients and buy the one with the shortest list.

+ Make it from scratch. Premade snacks and food often contain fillers and heavy preservatives.

By buying your own ingredients, you can easily make your favorite food at home. Plus, you'll have a new skill under your belt that will inevitably come in handy.

Grow Your Own Herbs

This is perhaps the easiest way to make sure your herbs are of good quality and ethically harvested. However, it's not always the most accessible. It took me YEARS to grow my own herbs, as I moved so often and couldn't keep a plant of any kind alive. Do a quick search for what herbs grow best in pots, or if you have the space, make a small garden and grow the herbs that you want most. You can do this! If I can grow herbs, anyone can.

Storing Fresh Herbs and Flowers

Keeping herbs and edible flowers fresh and pretty can be tricky. I can't even tell you how many times I've nearly cried over a spoiled batch of flowers that I didn't get to in time to cook with. It's a lot, though. Over the years, I've figured out a few nifty tricks to extend the life of my foraged or market finds in the fridge.

Plastic Bags: We all have plastic shopping bags kicking around in some dark corner of our kitchen. I will often harvest herbs or flowers with a plastic bag in tow and just toss them in there as I harvest. Tie the bag by the handles and keep it in your fridge. This method really extends the life of herbs and flowers.

Water Jars: Treat your fresh herbs like flowers and store them in jars of water in the fridge. Plus, it looks beautiful and picture worthy. #fridgeshot Add a resealable plastic bag or small paper bag over herb tops for extra protection.

Containers and Towels: Most of the time, condensation will be the death of your herbs or flowers. Line a glass, plastic, or paper container with a paper or cloth towel before adding the fresh plants. Make sure to seal well.

Bowl of Water: Fill a bowl with water and lay the flowers on top of the water. Gently lay a towel over the bowl and place it in the fridge. Flower cereal!

Pantry Essentials

Once upon a time, my only pantry essentials were a large bottle of sriracha, an onion or two, and some twenty-nine-cent ramen. Though these are still vital in my pantry, I've opened my heart and cupboard doors to many other delicious goods. My favorite thing about cooking is that there are so many things to experiment with, learn from, and make yours in your own special way. These are a few of my favorite things that I've pared down over the years and keep on hand at all times.

Bouillon: Get it in a jar or cubed. I use some bullion when I don't have broth, or I'll add a tiny bit to whatever I'm cooking to add extra flavor. I don't have a particular brand that I lean toward, but I do prefer veggie- or mushroom-based bouillon, as it's more versatile and suits the range of my friends' palates.

Butter: I overcame my aversion to cooking with butter back in herb school. It wasn't anything in particular that made me resist it (well, maybe '90s diet culture), but I had gotten used to cooking with oil, so I'd never given it much thought. At the moment, I have a mass quantity of unsalted Kerrygold butter in my fridge, and it's my go-to for whatever I make. It doesn't matter whether I'm cooking with ghee (page 30) or a healthy slab of butter. I always suggest cooking and baking with unsalted butter so you can better control the salt level. Save the salted stuff for slathering on bread or baked goods.

Cane Sugar: I rarely ever use granulated table sugar in my food. In fact, it's the only ingredient that I'm majorly insistent upon and even pains me if I need to use anything but. I love the flavor of cane sugar and never have had an issue with it while baking. There's a great depth of flavor with cane sugar that you can't get with white granulated sugar and that can't be beaten. I buy it in five-pound bags from Walmart that last me for at least three months at a time. However, you can use honey as a sweetener in place of sugar in any of these recipes.

Canned Beans: I'm not a snob when it comes to my beans. Give 'em to me canned or dried and I'll make the best bean dish I possibly can. But for the sake of ease, I like them canned. Just make sure to give them a good rinse before use and buy low sodium if you can.

Canned Tomatoes: I live in Montana, and we don't get the greatest-looking tomatoes year round. I discovered the joy of cooking with canned tomatoes my first year in Montana, and I haven't looked back since. And trust me—once you figure out a good recipe for homemade pasta sauce, you'll avoid the jarred stuff. Look for tomatoes with no salt added or low sodium. That way you have control over your salt intake.

Crackers: Listen, crackers are a joy in this world and a perfect vessel for most foods. I like to keep a box of buttery club crackers or saltines in my pantry at all times. Luckily, crackers are made to suit all sorts of diets now, so you can find a good box to suit your own needs.

Coconut Milk or Heavy Cream: You may be wondering whether these two things have any similarities, and, to me, they definitely do. Adding coconut milk or heavy cream to your cooking will instantly add a satisfying creaminess. And in many cases, it can help cover up an oversalted dish. Just make sure to get full-fat coconut milk for the most delicious flavor.

Dried Herbs: From thyme and oregano to tulsi and nettles, having a good selection of dried herbs in your kitchen is key. Buy small amounts of culinary or medicinal herbs and experiment with them in your food. Find what tastes best to you and keep some in a jar or shaker for easy access while you cook.

Herbal Flours/Powders: Keeping various jars of herbal powders in the pantry is a must for me in my little herby kitchen. There's a wide variety of powdered herb products on the market these days, and I've listed a few of my favorites on page 200. They are also very easy to make, and you can find more info on page 121.

Hot Sauce: From sriracha to Louisiana hot sauce, I always have some sort of hot sauce in my house. In my early twenties, it was common knowledge among my friends that sriracha could be found on my bedside table, since I ate most of my meals in bed at the time. Hot sauce spices up any meal and can add depth to an accidentally bland dish.

Kosher Salt: For me, cooking with anything but kosher salt isn't going to happen. If you've read Samin Nosrat's *Salt Fat Acid Heat*, you may know a thing or two about the wonders of kosher salt. It's not as salty as your typical table salt, which gives you more control as you cook. I prefer the Diamond Crystal brand because I like how easily it folds into food, but grab whatever you can find. Skip the shakers and keep salt in a jar or bowl next to your stove for easy access.

Nutritional Yeast: If you've ever experimented with plant-based eating, you know nutritional yeast is a staple. I like to keep some on hand because I love the flavor and it truly does make a decent cheese substitute. I have a theory that adding a tablespoon of nutritional yeast to roasted potatoes will help achieve the perfect amount of crispness. As I said, this is just a theory, but every time I roast potatoes, I've been proven right, so... do with that what you will.

Oils: This is a given, but having a good cooking oil makes a world of difference, and having a range of oils on hand will open up endless possibilities. And, hey, if good-quality oil isn't in your budget, don't feel bad for buying the cheap stuff; however, I will recommend getting extra-virgin olive oil if possible. I also like to keep a neutral oil, like canola or vegetable, on hand for frying purposes. By using a neutral-tasting oil for frying, you're not overpowering your food with the flavor of the oil.

Peppercorn: Pre-ground pepper is not typically something that has a place in my kitchen. To fully appreciate the flavor and medicinal benefits of pepper, you have to buy it whole. Invest in a simple pepper grinder (I found mine at a thrift shop) and keep it full at all times. You can find peppercorn in the spice section at your market, or you can go fancy and buy it at a specialty store.

Red Pepper Flakes: I buy these from the bulk section and store them in a Mason jar directly above my stove for easy access. Red pepper flakes offer a depth of spice without overpowering the flavor, like most hot sauces.

Rose Petals: I can't express how much I think you should start adding rose petals to your food. They add a very subtle yet noticeable flavor to any meal that will definitely impress your guests. I add rose petals to salads, creamy pasta, and baked goods. Make sure to add them last because high heat will damage the delicate petals and wreck the taste. You can find dried rose petals at a natural food market or herb shop. There is also a list of online resources on page 199.

Sour Cream: Connor, my husband, often jokes that I'm a sour cream addict. While this may or may not be true (it definitely is), I think using sour cream is always a good idea. It can be used to add creaminess to soups and sauces or to make a salad dressing. One of my favorite tricks is mixing it with spices and fresh herbs to make a dip (see page 61). A good, thick full-fat yogurt will also work in place of sour cream.

Tinned Fish: I often joke that fish swim in my blood thanks to my Celtic and Scandinavian ancestry. I've been a sucker for tinned fish for as long as I can remember. To me, there's something romantic about tinned fish. I love knowing that it can sustain and nourish me comfortably while being inexpensive and shelf stable. Get some anchovies, smoked mussels, and a good can of tuna for your own pantry. Fishwife makes some of my favorite canned smoked fish. They are women owned, and sustainable fishing is a big part of their platform, which I love. Wild Planet and Bar Harbor are also great options and have a good variety of products. I like to break open a can of sardines or smoked cockles to eat with club crackers when I need an easy dinner. And don't knock anchovies until you've cooked them with butter and smeared them on a hunk of crusty bread topped with fresh parsley. I keep it simple with Roland or Cento brands since it's what we have at our local market. But if you're new to anchovies and using only a few at a time, buy jarred. That way you can use one or two, pop the lid back on, and save the rest for later.

Tomato Paste: From soups to sauce, tomato paste is a must for me. It's the perfect addition to every tomato dish and can be used to add a dash of color to your food. Get it tubed or in a little can. I typically buy whatever is on sale.

Essential Kitchen Tools

These are a few of my favorite things to keep handy in the kitchen at all times. I like to keep my kitchen simple and use mostly secondhand tools whenever possible. I grew up with my chef dad dragging me to all sorts of kitchen supply stores. Before getting on the boat to Nantucket, we'd always have to stop at the supply store in Hyannis, and while I probably made a stink about being bored, I was always taken with the varieties of funny-shaped salt and pepper shakers and egg timers. It clearly made an impression on me, as my search for the perfect set of tongs or a well-made spatula has become my passion in life.

My dad is a no-frills sort of chef and a firm believer in buying secondhand as well. This is something I have come to deeply appreciate, and most of my well-loved kitchen goods are from thrift shops, free piles, or yard sales. Not only are vintage tools made to last but also they are full of character and look good on a countertop. However, I tend to avoid used plastic or well-used wooden tools, since both hold on to smells and stains easily. If you feel weird about a particular secondhand gadget, you will most likely never reach for it. Waste o' space.

Butter Knives: I love wooden butter knives and use them for an array of foods. The wide paddle shape is perfect for scooping and spreading. Whenever I see a butter knife on a table, I know I'm about to enjoy some good food.

Knives: I'm still trying to figure out my knife game. I love good paring knives, and I use the classic black-handled kitchen knife that my dad gave me when I moved to Portland. Just make sure to keep your knives sharp and you (most likely) won't have an issue. Buy a simple kitchen knife sharpener or find a local "knife person" who will do a professional job on your precious knives.

Kitchen Shears: Keep a sturdy pair of scissors in your kitchen and use them only for food-related things. I have a tendency to squirrel scissors away, so I always try to keep some exclusively in my workstation.

Tongs: Spend your money on a good pair of tongs; I use mine for almost everything. You want to make sure that they grip well and don't get stuck in the open or closed position easily. I love to keep it simple with metal tongs. You can find these at any kitchen supply or box store.

Bench Scraper: Bench scrapers are an important tool to clean up a messy countertop or move cut veggies to a pan. I have a few different ones that I keep right below my workstation. I prefer plastic scrapers, as they are compact and so easy to clean.

Cheese Slicer: This is a pretty standard Swedish tool and one that I grew up with. It helps cut thinner, more even slices and can act as a spatula when your actual spatula is dirty in the sink.

Pastry Brush: These little brushes really come in handy and are something I consider essential when baking. There's really nothing else that can replace a pastry brush when you need to brush an egg wash on dough. I prefer the silicone brushes over the traditional wooden ones, as they are easier to clean.

Rolling Pins: I have two rolling pins in my kitchen. The first one, a wedding gift, weighs about three pounds and is useful for tough doughs. The second is a lightweight Betty Crocker wooden rolling pin that I found at the dollar store. It's the one I use most, and I absolutely adore it. Every so often, I'll hit it with some oil to extend the life, but I've had it for four years and it's still going. I use only tapered rolling pins.

Whisks: Get a good 10-inch whisk and keep it close. I use a silicone whisk with a wooden handle, as I find that the silicone ones are easier to clean. I also keep a mini whisk in a cup on my countertop. Mini whisks are helpful for small tasks like whisking eggs or tiny bowls of sauce.

Wooden Spoons: Bamboo is what I usually lean toward for wooden spoons, as they are cheaper and last quite a few years longer. Just make sure you don't let wooden spoons soak in water for too long, as the wood can split and possibly mold.

Spider Strainer: I honestly can't believe I went so long without one of these bad boys. Spider strainers are ideal for boiling eggs, frying, or draining pasta and veggies. For the most part, spider strainers eliminate the need for a full colander and take up way less space. (Can you tell that space-saving tools are a requirement in my tiny kitchen?) I prefer the bamboo-handled ones, which you can find at any Asian market.

Handheld Strainers: Everyone has their favorite colander/strainer. Mine is a simple handheld strainer from Ikea. It's not fancy, but it's easy to clean and hangs out of the way on my wall. I use mine for everything from straining herbal syrups or tinctures to making my favorite boxed mac 'n' cheese.

Handheld Mixer: I have both an immersion blender and a handheld mixer. When you live small, you learn how to cook without a stand-up mixer. I've never felt the need to own one and have done fine with my little handheld guys.

Lots of Good Cutting Boards: I have about six cutting boards, and I use every single one of them. Most are wood, but I keep a big plastic cutting board for when we process meat or fish.

An Assortment of Mixing Bowls: This is my vintage weakness; however, I've gotten really good at paring down what I need versus what I don't. Make sure your bowls are light enough that they aren't painful to clean.

Pots and Pans: The most expensive pan I have is stainless steel, and it's already misshapen. I tend to stick with heavy-bottomed vintage pieces I've spent years collecting or the true copper pots and pans I inherited from my grandmother. If scouring thrift shops isn't your thing, eBay and Esty have amazing deals on old Dutch ovens, pots, and pans. Lodge is my favorite brand when buying new. It's always good quality, inexpensive, and will last forever. Cast-iron pans are also heavily used in our house because they are so versatile and can be used on the stove, in the oven, or over a fire.

Now that we've covered some of my favorite herbs to cook with, pantry and tool essentials, and some other basics, we can create some fabulous dishes. I like to organize recipes seasonally because I feel that it's important to pay attention to what is in season and what plants grow during that time. This allows you to create a sort of relationship with the world around you and see what pops up as the seasons change. You'll notice that dandelion recipes are concentrated in the spring because that's when they begin to show up in our yards. In fall and winter, I work with roots and herbs that are easily preserved in the warmer months for colder ones. Every region has a different climate and growing season, so getting to know your own location is key to finding what foods are in season around you and what makes your belly the happiest. Garnishes also change seasonally so don't be afraid to stray from my suggestions by adding what you have available. I keep dried herbs and flowers on hand to brighten up dishes in the winter months. Have fun and never ever be afraid to experiment with new foods!

Spring

The First Foray into Spring

Seeley Lake, Montana

We've found a spot down a red dirt road that looks just about right. My husband, Connor, parks the van, and we set up the table beneath a nearby tree. As Connor begins collecting kindling for a fire, I pour myself a cup of red wine and start exploring our immediate area. I keep my eyes downcast in hopes of seeing signs of ground life—a small patch of nettles or the elusive morel— but it's not quite that time yet in Montana. It's early May. The ground is still hard, and the brush that slept beneath the snow is just now returning to its green state. A patch of sun peaks through the trees, so I stand and move my face toward it—a firm decision to stand in silence and little thought.

This is our first time back out in the van since November. Still a bit rusty, we forgot our camp stove at home, so we'll be forging ahead with a makeshift grill over a damp fire pit. We bought bologna and cheese for sandwiches at the market in town just in case we can't get the fire to start, but we're hopeful. You've always got to be hopeful when you're planning a stay in the forest. Nature is not that dependable.

Before we attempt the fire, we sit. Not many words are exchanged, and no podcast or music is playing. We're practicing idleness, something that is almost unfathomable in this modern culture. It feels uncomfortable, and there is a little part of me that doesn't know what to do with myself. I listen for what's nearby: a few birds, the flop of a trout, the people at a site not so far away. I hear something resembling the snort of some sort of animal and cautiously stand up to scan my surroundings and investigate. If it was a bear or a deer, it's out of sight for now. But, more likely, it's our old van making some strange settling noise.

I stand up once again and walk to the edge of the lake. I contemplate a swim but turn back when the air sends a slight chill across my shoulders. I return to my half-broken camp chair and make a mental note to pull some tarot cards before dinner. It's been almost a full season since I've touched any of my decks, and today feels like the right time. Later, when I've pulled my card, I flip it over to find the Seven of Wands looking back at me. It's an indication that I've taken on too much within myself. Mindless noise on a mountain of busywork, useless chatter and criticism in my own head. The Seven of Wands is a reminder to not take on so much and pull a few things off my plate or, at least, set them aside for the time being. Being in this world is hard enough, and it's not entirely necessary to say and do such mean things to yourself or take on a lot of work to feel like you aren't being lazy. Idleness is an uncomfortable feeling, and being in nature can also be uncomfortable. But there was a time when humans were always in nature. Once you've found your way back to the quiet and the trees, it gets easier to feel at home. Nature can embrace you and feel as comforting as a slow-cooked meal if you let yourself be present for it. Trust me (and the trees!) on that.

Dandelion Greens with Molasses and Onions

Serves 1 to 2

2 tablespoons unsalted
butter or ghee (page 30)

1 large yellow onion, cut
into 1-inch slices

8 ounces fresh
dandelion greens

1 tablespoon molasses

3 cloves garlic, minced

Salt and freshly ground
black pepper

Red pepper flakes

This is a simple recipe with a lot of heart. I made this a lot when I lived in a tiny farmhouse attic in Maine back in 2016. Since then, I like to make this dish whenever I'm struggling with poor digestion or I want to feel closer to the earth. Dandelion greens are packed full of nutrients and can be such a wonderful aid for digestion and bloating. These days, fresh dandelion greens can be found in many markets in the produce section, typically near the lettuce and other leafy greens. Of course, if you aren't able to find them in stores or aren't able to forage them from a pesticide-free area, you can always substitute a different green. I've made this recipe with rainbow chard, and it would also be lovely with some mustard greens. Like most greens, the dandelion will shrink a good amount during the cooking process. If you want to make a larger batch, double the number of greens and molasses used. You can also use honey instead of molasses if that's what you have on hand. Red chili flakes also make a great addition to this recipe if you want to add spice. Serve this dish warm on toast with goat cheese or as a side to your favorite comfort food. I personally love pairing dandelion leaves with a healthy portion of baked beans.

✦ ✦ ✦

Place the butter in a large pan over medium heat. Once the butter has melted, add the onion. Cook the onions for 8 to 10 minutes, until soft and translucent.

While the onions are cooking, rinse the dandelion greens and remove about ½ inch from the stems. Cut the whole bunch into thirds and place into the pan with the onions.

Add the molasses and garlic, then season the greens to your liking with salt, pepper, and red pepper flakes. Cook for 8 to 10 minutes, until the greens have wilted and the stems have become soft. Serve warm.

Ghee

Makes about 2 cups

1 pound unsalted butter

I learned how to make ghee during herb school, and I remember being enthralled and totally mind blown once I tasted it for the first time. Ghee has a comforting and creamy, nutty flavor that is perfect for slathering on toast or dropping a tablespoon in some homemade broth (page 175). Making it yourself is very cost effective, too, since jars of the good stuff typically cost $11 or more in stores. Ghee has a distinct role in Ayurvedic medicine thanks to its healthy fat content and easily digestible properties. One of my favorite Ayurvedic practices is called Netra Basti, which is essentially a ghee bath for your eyes (trust me, it feels AMAZING). It's safe to say ghee goes a long way. It also has a high smoke point, which makes it perfect for use in place of cooking oil.

+ + +

Place the butter in a medium heavy-bottomed pot over medium heat. Once the butter has melted and started to simmer, decrease the heat to medium-low. You'll notice the top of the ghee begin to get a bit frothy and white. Keep simmering on low for 15 to 20 minutes, until it has become clear and you notice milk solids on the bottom of the pan. It will also have a nutty flavor at this point. Remove the pot from the heat and strain the liquid through a finely woven handheld strainer into a clean pint-sized jar. Let it cool before capping the jar tightly. Keep the ghee on the countertop for 2 weeks or in the fridge for 1 month.

Creamy Adaptogenic Avocado Dip

Serves 8 to 10

1 ripe avocado, halved, skin removed, and pitted

Juice of ½ orange

2 cloves garlic

1 cup raw cashews, soaked overnight in water and drained, liquid discarded

2 tablespoons extra-virgin olive oil

1 tablespoon maca powder

¼ teaspoon cayenne pepper

1 cup water

Salt and freshly ground black pepper

I originally made this as a salad dressing for a cooking class I taught awhile back. I didn't anticipate how thick it would turn out, so I thought quickly and changed it to a dip at the last moment before the class. To this day, it's probably the best mistake I've ever made. This dip is absolutely stunning and so simple to make. It goes well with basically anything too. You can add more water to thin this dip and use it as a dressing for salads.

Place the avocado in a blender or food processor with all the other ingredients. Make sure to taste as you go so you can get a sense of what tastes best to you. Add more garlic, orange juice, or water if needed. They're your taste buds, baby! Enjoy what you eat.

Marmee's Lavender Limoncello

Makes about 2½ liters

20 Meyer lemons, cleaned

1 (1.75-liter) bottle vodka or Everclear

2 cups Lavender Simple Syrup (page 85)

When I was seventeen, I was lucky enough to spend the summer in Italy with my oldest friend, Maria. Her mother is Italian, and Maria had spent a few years attending high school just outside of Rome. We hatched the plan over the phone and letters and pitched the idea to our parents, who thankfully agreed that it would probably be good for the two of us. While much of the trip was made up of the shenanigans of two American teenagers running around a foreign country, we did manage to get some good sightseeing and culture in. I fondly remember the tall bottles of limoncello that lined the shelves of every touristy corner store. I bought a whole new suitcase just to fit all the mirto, bottles of two-euro wine, and, of course, limoncello to take back to Nantucket with me.

This is my mom's (whom I sometimes call "marmee," à la Little Women, which is our favorite story) recipe for an easy at-home limoncello. I, of course, added the lavender simple syrup because I have to find some way to make everything herby. I like to make this in late winter/ early spring, when the Meyer lemons are still going strong, and it allows plenty of time for infusion. The longer you let the lemon vodka infuse, the more yellow and tasty it will be. Keep the limoncello chilled and sip in the summer when the days are long and hot.

Use a rasp grater to finely zest the lemons into a large bowl. Place the zest in a wide-mouth gallon-sized jar and cover with the vodka. Cap the container and let the mixture infuse for 2 to 3 weeks in the dark, at room temperature.

After 2 to 3 weeks it'll be time to make the simple syrup. Strain the lemon zest into a large bowl and transfer the liquid back to the jar. Combine the simple syrup and vodka. Stir well. Transfer to clean jars or bottles or keep in the original container. Store in the fridge or a dark cupboard. The limoncello will keep for up to 1 year.

Mushroomy Shakshuka

Serves 2 to 4

1 tablespoon
unsalted butter or
extra-virgin olive oil

1 small yellow onion,
chopped into 1-inch pieces

2 cups beech mushrooms

1 tablespoon honey

1 teaspoon
balsamic vinegar

1 teaspoon
smoked paprika

1 tablespoon
minced garlic

1 (14.5-ounce) can
diced tomatoes,
preferably unsalted

1 tomato, diced, or 1 cup
cherry tomatoes, chopped

Salt and freshly
ground black pepper

4 large eggs

Dill flowers, calendula,
fresh violet leaves, or
lemon balm, for garnish

Soft chèvre or feta,
for serving

Crusty loaf of bread,
for serving

I discovered shakshuka a few years ago and quickly became obsessed. Shakshuka is a popular Middle Eastern dish that is well deserving of its icon status. Whenever I have mushrooms in the fridge that need to be used up, this is one of my go-to dishes. I like the look and taste of beech mushrooms (they're so darn cute), but you can use whatever mushrooms you have on hand. Just make sure you don't crowd the mushrooms in the pan, as this causes them to steam and retain more water. You want them to brown and get a little crispy. Regarding the herbs and cheese used in this recipe, it's up to your preference. I like to cover my shakshuka with lots of mint, violet leaves, and cheese. So I'm going to leave this bit up to you. But, really, you can never have too much of those things, right? Serve with a crusty loaf of bread and a good bottle of saison.

✦ ✦ ✦

Place the butter in a medium cast-iron pan (nonstick works too) over medium heat. Once the butter has melted, add the onions and mushrooms and sauté for 8 to 10 minutes, until the mushrooms have browned and the onions have become soft and translucent.

Add the honey, vinegar, paprika, and garlic, then stir until the honey has melted. Pour in the canned tomatoes and add the fresh tomatoes. Season to your liking with salt and pepper and let simmer for 12 to 15 minutes, until the tomato juices have evaporated.

Crack the eggs into the tomato mixture, then either cover the pan with a lid or place it in an oven preheated to 350°F. Cook the eggs for 5 to 7 minutes, until the whites have set. Once the eggs have set, remove the pan from heat. Top the eggs with your desired amount of herb or flower garnishes of choice. Serve warm with soft cheese and a crusty loaf of bread for dipping.

Ginger French Toast with Marmalade Cream

Serves 3 to 4

Marmalade Cream

2 tablespoons orange marmalade

1 teaspoon cane sugar (optional)

½ cup heavy whipping cream

French Toast

3 large eggs

1 cup whole milk

3 tablespoons maple syrup or other sugar

2 tablespoons grated fresh ginger

1 teaspoon vanilla extract

2 tablespoons butter, divided

8 to 10 (1-inch) slices day-old baguette

I like to reserve this recipe for when I have a baguette that has aged a day or two—which happens more often than I like to admit. But, of course, you can always use fresh bread. Aside from making them at home (which is rare for me to do), our nearest option for a good baguette is thirty minutes away. My favorite Missoula bakery, Le Petit Outre, luckily delivers to the town over from mine, so I'll often have Connor pick up a loaf or two on his way home from work. This breakfast feels whimsical and reminds me of something you'd find in a classic children's book about gardens and talking animals. So put on your finest threads, lay out your favorite antique tablecloth, pour yourself a cup of milky tea, and enjoy the morning as you eat this.

+ + +

To make the marmalade cream, place the marmalade, sugar, if using, and cream in a medium bowl. Using a whisk or a handheld mixer, whip the cream until it forms stiff peaks. Serve right away or keep covered in the fridge for 2 to 3 days. I usually store whipped cream in the bowl I made it in, with plastic wrap pressed down onto the surface of the cream to prevent separation and a film from forming on the top.

To make the French toast, crack the eggs into a large bowl and beat until smooth. Then add the milk, maple syrup, ginger, and vanilla to the bowl, whisking until well combined. Heat a medium pan over medium heat and melt 1 tablespoon of the butter. Place 3 to 4 slices at a time into the egg mix and completely coat the bread. Transfer the coated slices to the pan. Cook the bread for 2 minutes on each side, or until crispy and golden brown. Once done, move the bread to a clean serving platter and cover with a kitchen towel or aluminum foil to keep warm. Repeat the process with the remaining bread slices, starting with melting the remaining tablespoon of butter. Serve warm with marmalade cream and/or maple syrup.

Premixed Golden Milk

Makes 20 to 25 servings, depending on how much you use at a time

1 cup turmeric

¼ cup ground ginger

¼ cup ground cardamom

1 tablespoon ground cinnamon

1 tablespoon ashwagandha or other herbal powder

1 teaspoon black pepper

¼ tablespoon salt

½ to 1 cup cane sugar (optional)

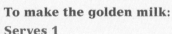

Golden milk is an ancient Indian and Ayurvedic remedy to aid inflammation, promote sleep, soothe sore throats, and prevent colds. Traditionally known as simply "turmeric milk," golden milk is a frothy, extremely Westernized version of the classic drink. It's delicious and packed full of herby, spicy goodness.

This mix is ideal for forest adventures. I like to make a batch to keep in my cupboard for use at home and toss the jar in my pack when I'm heading outside for the day. Add a tablespoon or two to heated-up milk of your choice et voilà! You've got yourself a healing cup of goodness to cozy up with on your couch or by the fire pit. This also makes a great addition to baked goods, pasta, rice, etc.

+ + +

Place all the ingredients in a quart-sized jar. Cap tightly and shake until well combined. This will keep on your spice rack for up to 6 months.

To make the golden milk:
Serves 1

Place 1½ cups of your preferred milk in a small saucepan over low heat. Bring the milk to a light simmer and add 1 tablespoon of the powdered mix. Using a whisk or handheld frother, mix until well combined and smooth. Continue heating the milk and add sweetener if desired. Once everything is combined and to your liking, remove the pan from the heat and serve the milk hot. This can also be cooled and served over ice.

The Nettle Harvest

Sonoma County, California

The air felt salty and lilac as I navigated my way through the nettles. The stalks were tall and just as good as gone to seed, but I was determined to see my plan through. It was 2013, and there seemed to be an abundance of supermoons that year. This backyard journey of mine was taking place under the ripest side of the moon. I could feel some strange wave pulsing through me as I waved my scissors in front of me to sort of form a path through the nettles, as if the brandishing of hard metal and plastic would ease the inevitable sting.

It was somewhat of a rush job. Considering the age of this nettle patch (they are best harvested before going to seed), I needed to harvest them sooner rather than later. I had procrastinated enough already. At 5'4", the stalks had grown well to my elbows, and the leaves brushed against the length of my legs. I've never been one to shy away from the sting of a nettle, so I chose to embrace the minimal stinging as I collected. Once I filled my brown paper shopping bag with the greens, I pocketed my shears and looked up at the moon as if thanking her for guidance through the tall patch.

As I made my way back to my redwood cabin, with the golden orb of a moon rising in front of me, the sting began to settle in. Rising up through my calves, thighs, and belly, I felt as if the nettles were captivating my whole being in a way I hadn't experienced before. While not painful, the feeling was overwhelming. I pulled my old Subaru to the side of the road to call my friend and herb school classmate Kelley. She assured me that all was going to be okay and that the feeling of being overwhelmed would cease. Kelley told me to go home, make some tea, and sit on my porch. I felt heady and spacey as I hung up the phone with her. After a few minutes, I started my car and started the short journey home. I did as Kelley instructed. I boiled some water, infused a few herbs, and sat under the heavy redwoods that surrounded my tiny home. I stared at the moon, sipped my tea, and let myself feel grounded once again.

The reason for this feeling was due to something called urtication. As you may already know, stinging nettles do, in fact, sting. The little hairs on the leaves and stems, when in contact with skin, can be irritating and long lasting in some cases. I, on the other hand, sort of enjoy it. Rather, it doesn't irritate me as much as it "should," I suppose. It feels as though something is working its way into my bloodstream, swarming inflammation and stimulating it enough to decrease. Urtication is the practice of flogging yourself or another willing participant in order to cease inflammatory pain. From helping with arthritis to easing back pain and swollen joints, this practice has been used and studied for years—once again proving the magic and healing benefits of nettles.

✤ ✤ ✤

Please be sure to consult a medical professional before beginning any new practice or herbal routine.

Blanching Nettles

Blanching nettles is one of the easiest ways to save full nettle leaves for later kitchen use. This is a necessary step for cooking with freshly harvested nettles, as blanching the leaves removes the sting. I repeat: this is a very important step when eating fresh nettle leaves! If you don't take the time to blanch fresh nettles, the sting will remain, and no one wants a tingly tongue. You can use blanched nettles right away or freeze them to use at a later time. This blanching and freezing method can be applied to most leafy green herbs.

Step-by-Step Guide

1: While wearing gloves, snip the nettle leaves from the stems and set them aside in a bag or large bowl. Compost the stems.

2: Fill a large pot halfway with water and bring to a roaring boil over high heat.

3: Add the nettle leaves to the boiling water. Using a wooden spoon or tongs, submerge the nettles.

4: Boil the nettles for 1 to 2 minutes, stirring often.

5: Using tongs or a spider strainer, remove the nettles from the water and place them in a clean bowl. Let cool.

6: Once cool, place the nettles in freezer-safe containers or bags. Divide into any amount you'd like. Nettles will keep in the freezer for up to 6 months.

Strain the leftover nettle water through a fine-mesh strainer to drink as an infusion or add to an herb broth. You can also pour the nettle water into an ice cube mold, freeze, and add to iced tea.

Nettle Soup

Serves 6

¼ cup (½ stick) unsalted butter or ghee

½ pound Yukon gold potatoes, peeled and chopped into 2-inch chunks

½ large yellow onion, coarsely chopped

Salt and freshly ground black pepper

4 cups Plant Magic Broth (page 175)

1 cup frozen nettles, or 2½ cups fresh nettles, rinsed

1 tablespoon thyme

7 sage leaves

4 to 5 cloves garlic, coarsely chopped

1 teaspoon red pepper flakes

1 cup full-fat coconut milk

Crème fraîche

Clover blossom, for garnish

There's truly nothing better than a good bowl of creamy soup. I would undoubtedly eat soup every day, no matter the season, if I could. It's basically just sauce that's acceptable to eat with a spoon, and you know I love a good sauce. This nettle soup is one of my favorite soups to date. Plus, it's full of nettles, which means that it's packed with nutrients and earthy magic. You can use blanched and frozen nettles (page 40) or fresh nettles straight from the ground. Just make sure to remove the stems and give the nettles a good rinse to get rid of any bugs before cooking with them. You'll find nettles in spring or early summer, depending on where you are.

I use my immersion blender to puree soups right in the pan, but you can also use a blender and mix in batches. Serve warm with a dollop of Herbed Sour Cream (page 61) or Herbed Croutons (page 125). PS. This soup is nice and thick, so you can even use it as a sauce over some pasta.

+ + +

Place the butter in a large pot over medium heat. Once the butter has melted, add the potatoes and onions. Season with a little bit of salt and cook over medium heat for 12 to 15 minutes, until the potatoes can be easily pierced with a fork and the onions are soft and translucent.

Add the broth, nettles, thyme, sage, garlic, and red pepper flakes to the pot and season with salt to taste. Simmer for 10 minutes, add the coconut milk, and simmer for another 10 minutes, stirring occasionally. Remove the pot from the heat. Using an immersion blender, puree the soup. Once done pureeing, add your desired amount of pepper and more salt if needed. Gently stir in some crème fraîche, top with a clover blossom, and serve warm.

Nettle Crackers

Makes about 30 crackers

3 cups all-purpose flour

2 teaspoons cane sugar

2 teaspoons salt

1 heaping tablespoon
dried nettles

4 tablespoons extra-
virgin olive oil

1 cup water

½ cup seeds, your choice,
or Everything Bagel
and Herbs Seasoning
(page 185)

It took me a long time to realize how easy it is to make crackers in your own kitchen. It's faster than you'd expect, and making them at home allows you control over the spices, ingredients, and salt you add. Crackers are also pretty darn expensive, so learning how to bake your own can be really helpful if you're on a budget. Either way, this is a simple way to start building up your easy-peasy baking go-tos. I like to scatter the Everything Bagel and Herbs Seasoning (page 185) over the dough before baking. I serve these with cheese or any kind of dip, like the Creamy Adaptogenic Avocado Dip (page 31).

+ + +

Preheat the oven to 450°F.

Place the flour, sugar, salt, and nettles in a medium bowl and mix. Add 1 tablespoon each olive oil and water at a time while mixing continuously. Continue adding 1 tablespoon oil and water at a time, mixing with your hands until the dough is shaggy in texture. You may not need to use all of the water. Gently knead the dough in the bowl with your hands.

Once the dough has formed, dump it onto a large floured surface and shape it into a ball. Roll the dough out into one thin sheet, about ⅛ inch thick. Brush the dough with about 1 tablespoon water and sprinkle with the seeds or seasoning. Cut the dough into your desired shape using a pizza cutter or cookie cutter. Line a baking sheet with parchment paper. Place the crackers on the baking sheet.

Bake for 12 to 14 minutes, until the edges have browned slightly. Let cool. Store in an airtight container for up to 1 week. These can also be stored in an airtight container in the freezer for up to 2 months.

The New Moon Circle

Nantucket, Massachusetts

My friend Lindsey's Sprinter van barrels up Nantucket's narrow Centre Street. I'm waiting in front of a blooming lilac bush and jump eagerly into the passenger seat once she stops. We're heading out to a friend's house in Madaket to celebrate May's new moon in Taurus around a fire with some friends. Lindsey is about seven months pregnant, and the massive size of the van she's driving engulfs her. I'm impressed that she can drive this thing so casually.

We drive toward Madaket, on the eastern side of the island. I love this side because the stars are usually in full effect out here, but tonight is different. Clouds form in the sky as the sun sets, and the air, while warm, is whipping around us with ferocity. Once we arrive at our friend's house, the fire pit is waiting with a pile of dry wood and paper stacked in the center. This is my first time at this particular monthly gathering, and I feel a bit awkward, so I take a seat, help when asked, and manage the flowers that keep tipping over in their vases.

My awkwardness doesn't last long, though. Once the fire is a luscious blaze and everyone has found their seats, I feel calm again. It's been a long time since I've spent time with other women in a group setting, and I'm eager to see what this ceremony entails. What I find is that it mostly consists of laughter, vulnerability, and lots of wood for the fire. A plate of herbed Brie, crackers, and strawberries gets passed around as we share our grievances, fears, and victories. Intentions are spoken aloud, cards are pulled, and island-grown roses are tossed into the fire. I have a particularly vulnerable moment while reading the description for the card I pulled, but it feels amazing to speak so freely in front of this small group. I am emotionally enraptured in a way I haven't felt in years.

One of my favorite things about food is that it is made to be shared. We pass around plates, share bites, and remark on taste as we spend time around a table. Food is emotional and intuitive in ways that we don't even realize. Our bodies instinctively know what we need to consume, even when we don't immediately know it. We crave meat when we need iron or protein and citrus when we're low on vitamins. I once went through a phase where I had to put rose petals in nearly everything I ate. This was during herb school when I was moving through grief and clearly needed some emotional heart medicine. Once you start familiarizing yourself with plants, you may start getting cravings for certain herbs too. I think it's one of the rewarding gifts we can receive from plants.

4-Ingredient Peanut Butter–Ashwagandha Cookies

Makes 6 to 8 cookies

1 cup peanut butter, smooth or crunchy

½ cup cane sugar

1 large egg

1 tablespoon ashwagandha

Cookies are probably the greatest sweet of all time. Believe it or not, I don't have much of a sweet tooth, but I'll never say no to a well-made cookie. A few years ago, Connor and I went through a phase of making these easy peanut butter cookies two or three times a week. We couldn't get enough of them. These cookies are comforting, rich, and perfect for satisfying any late-night craving. Serve with a tall glass of milk or an ice-cold beer. You can add any herbal powder you have on hand. Since these are typically a before-bed treat, I like to use ashwagandha, as it can help bring about restful sleep.

+ + +

Preheat the oven to 350°F. Place all the ingredients in a medium bowl and mix to combine. Line a baking sheet with parchment paper. Drop large spoonfuls (about 2 tablespoons each) out onto the baking sheet, leaving 3 inches between each cookie. Flatten the cookies with a fork, pressing down again in the opposite direction to make a crisscross pattern.

Bake for 8 to 10 minutes, until the edges are golden brown. Make sure to pull the cookies out while still soft as they will harden as they cool. Let cool slightly before serving. These will keep in a resealable plastic bag or airtight container for up to 1 week.

Herbed Baked Brie

Serves 2 to 4

1 (16-ounce) Brie round

1 tablespoon
Herbes de Provence

1 tablespoon dried or
chopped fresh tulsi

1 teaspoon freshly
grated lemon zest

2 tablespoons honey,
divided

Salt and freshly
ground black pepper

Herbes de Provence

Crackers or bread,
for serving

Never in a million years did I expect to be sharing a baked Brie recipe for any cookbook of mine. Often, I feel like baked Brie is boring and has been done in a million different ways. While this is in no way revolutionary, it's become a surprising staple in my household these days. Connor and I like to make this cheese and serve it with some butter crackers or nettle crackers and a very hefty drizzle of honey and sprinkling of red pepper flakes and sit on our floor to devour the entire round for dinner. Freezing the cheese first helps it keep its shape while in the oven. If the Brie you use comes in one of those wooden rounds, bake it in that. You can also substitute Camembert instead of Brie if you'd like. To me, cheese is best when horribly stinky; I don't care what any of y'all say.

✦ ✦ ✦

Preheat the oven to 350°F.

Halve the Brie crosswise (like you would a bagel) and place the rounds in the freezer for 20 minutes.

In a small bowl, add the herbs, zest, 1 tablespoon of the honey, and salt and pepper and mix until combined. Remove the Brie from the freezer and brush the herb mixture over the rounds.

Set the rounds in a small baking dish and place it in the oven for 15 to 20 minutes, until the Brie has melted. Remove from the oven and let rest for at least 5 minutes. Drizzle with the remaining 1 tablespoon of honey and a sprinkle of Herbes de Provence. Serve warm with crackers or bread.

The Green Sauce

Serves 4 to 6

½ cup fresh basil, finely chopped, including stems

½ cup fresh lemon balm, finely chopped, including stems

1 tablespoon dried tulsi

1 heaping teaspoon calendula petals, fresh or dried

1 shallot, thinly sliced

½ cup extra-virgin olive oil

3 to 5 cloves garlic, minced

1 to 2 small red chilies, seeded and minced

2 tablespoons red wine vinegar

Salt and freshly ground black pepper

This is my take on the classic chimichurri. It's a beautiful way to use up your farmers' market or garden bounty and is so beyond easy to make. Add some extra olive oil and freeze in ice cube trays, then transfer to a resealable plastic bag for year-round use. You can also make this more traditional by substituting basil for cilantro. Serve this green sauce with pretty much everything. It's great atop grilled veggies or sardines and saltines. There's no wrong way to enjoy this one.

✛ ✛ ✛

Place the basil and lemon balm in a medium bowl, then add all the remaining ingredients. Mix well and season to your liking with salt and pepper. This will keep in an airtight container in the fridge for up to 1 week. It's best served at room temperature.

Fire Cider Dip

Makes 1½ cups

1 cup Greek yogurt

1 small shallot, minced

1 heaping tablespoon minced pickled jalapeños

2 to 4 cloves garlic (raw or roasted), minced

1 teaspoon minced fresh rosemary

1 teaspoon turmeric powder

½ teaspoon ground ginger

¼ teaspoon freshly ground black pepper

½ teaspoon horseradish powder

1 tablespoon apple cider vinegar

1 teaspoon maple syrup, agave, or honey

Salt

Freshly grated lemon zest, for garnish

I've been dreaming of this recipe for about four years, but it wasn't until this book that I finally decided to go ahead and actually make it. Fire cider is a notorious little beast in the herbal world. Popularized by herbalist queen Rosemary Gladstar in the '70s, fire cider gained the spotlight a few years ago when an East Coast company trademarked the name and began suing small herbal companies for use of the name. Luckily, because of three badass herbalists, Mary Blue, Kathi Langelier, and Nicole Telkes, fire cider was released from its trademarked name in 2019 and is now free once again. Pair this dip with Dandelion Hushpuppies (page 56) or the Perfect Roasted Potatoes (page 127).

+ + +

Place all the ingredients except for the salt and lemon zest in a small bowl. Mix until well combined.

Add salt to taste and continue to mix. Store in the fridge in an airtight container for up to 1 week. Garnish with the lemon zest before serving.

Caramelized Onion and Nettle Mac 'n' Cheese

Serves 6 to 8

1 pound penne pasta

1 tablespoon extra-virgin olive oil

1 large yellow onion, coarsely chopped

1 tablespoon balsamic vinegar

Salt and freshly ground black pepper

1 cup blanched or frozen nettles, or ¾ cup dried nettles

½ cup (1 stick) unsalted butter

¼ cup all-purpose flour

2 cups milk

2 to 4 cloves garlic, minced

1 tablespoon Dijon mustard

1 teaspoon Worcestershire sauce

2 cups shredded smoked Gouda cheese

2 cups shredded cheddar cheese

1 tablespoon honey

¾ cup grated Parmesan cheese

¾ cup bread crumbs

There truly is nothing better than mac 'n' cheese. To me it doesn't matter whether it's from a box, microwavable, or homemade—mac 'n' cheese is my number one comfort meal. Adding nettles is a really nice way to sneak in some herbs, and it really just makes it taste better. If you don't have fresh nettles, you can use a smaller amount of the dried plant. Just add the dried nettles into the onions during the cooking process so they have more time to rehydrate. Keep in mind that this is more of a light caramelization process for the onions. They are still a little sweet and absolutely delicious but not nearly as time consuming. I like to make my mac 'n' cheese in one pot (aside from the pasta pot) if I can help it, so starting the cooking process in a large pot or pan that is oven safe is key.

+ + +

Place the penne in a medium pot and cook according to the instructions on the back of the package. Once the pasta is done, drain it and set it aside.

Place the olive oil in a large heavy-bottomed pan over medium-low heat. Once hot, place the onions in the pan, making sure to coat them in the oil. Add the vinegar, season with salt and pepper, and cook for 15 to 18 minutes, stirring occasionally. If using dried nettles, add them about 8 minutes into the cooking process, adding an extra teaspoon of olive oil if the mixture seems too dry. Once the onions are browned and soft, transfer them to a clean plate and set aside.

Preheat the oven to 450°F. Using the same pot as the onions, turn the heat to low and melt the butter. Once the butter has melted, add the flour, 1 tablespoon at a time, making sure to whisk the mixture continuously. Once the mixture has become a paste-like consistency, add the milk, ½ cup at a time, whisking frequently. When the mixture has become smooth, mix in the garlic, Dijon, Worcestershire, and nettles (if using blanched and/or frozen ones). Stir well, making sure the nettles are well incorporated. Add the Gouda

and cheddar and stir until melted. Fold in the reserved onions and the honey and stir in the pasta until well coated. Taste and season with more salt and pepper to your liking. Sprinkle the Parmesan and bread crumbs over the mixture and place the pot in the oven. Bake for 20 minutes, until the top has browned slightly and the mac has set. Change the oven setting to broil for an additional 4 to 5 minutes to get the top extra crispy. Remove the pot from the oven and let the mac cool for 10 minutes before serving. This will keep in the fridge for up to 4 days.

Dandelion Hushpuppies

Makes 16 to 20 hushpuppies

2 cups vegetable or peanut oil (or any neutral oil suitable for frying)

1 cup yellow cornmeal

½ cup all-purpose flour

3 tablespoons dandelion petals

½ teaspoon freshly ground black pepper

1 teaspoon baking soda

2 tablespoons cane sugar

1 teaspoon chili powder

1½ teaspoons garlic powder

1 teaspoon salt

1 large egg

1 cup whole milk or buttermilk

1 tablespoon pickled jalapeños, minced

1 cup shredded Gouda cheese

Dill flowers, fennel fronds, or dandelion petals, for garnish

The first time I remember eating a hushpuppy was during my stint as a server at a restaurant in the Fruitvale neighborhood of Oakland. The Half Orange was the definition of a fusion restaurant. A mix of Mexican, Korean, and Southern food, the dishes were over the top, messy, and, to this day, some of the best food I've ever tasted. Sausage and kimchi were made in-house, and the beer selection was top notch—I credit this place for making me the beer snob I am today. Hushpuppies at the Half Orange were served piping hot and stuffed with house-made chorizo and sausage. I'd often order these alongside my shift beer after work or take them home to my room in West Oakland. I'd eat them in my bed at 1 a.m., depressed and tired but feeling slightly elevated by the wonders of hushpuppies. These dandelion hushpuppies are no different, and I hope they bring you immense joy, no matter where you are in the world. Serve the hushpuppies with coleslaw and the Fire Cider Dip (page 53).

When harvesting the dandelions for this recipe, make sure to remove all green parts. Pluck the yellow petals from the dandelion and inspect for debris or bugs. I always recommend rinsing foraged herbs, so be sure to do this before you pluck, when the flower is whole. Rinse the dandelions under gently running water or submerge them in a large bowl of water for 30 seconds, then drain and pat dry.

+ + +

Place the oil in a large heavy-bottomed pot and warm over medium-low heat. While the oil is heating, combine the cornmeal, flour, dandelion petals, pepper, baking soda, sugar, chili powder, garlic powder, and salt in a large bowl. Mix the ingredients until any clumps are gone and the mixture is well combined.

Next, fold in the egg, milk, jalapeños, and Gouda. Mix until incorporated, adding a little more milk if the batter is too dry.

Check the temperature using a candy thermometer and when the cooking oil has reached 350°F, you can start the frying process. Using two small spoons, scoop a rounded bit of batter with one spoon, then round and push off with the second spoon. Cook in batches and fry each hushpuppy for 4 to 5 minutes. Test the first couple of hushpuppies to double-check the cooking time, as it may vary depending on the temperature of the oil.

Line a large plate with paper towels. Using a spider strainer or slotted spoon, transfer the hushpuppies to the plate. Repeat the process with the remaining batter. Garnish with dill flowers, fennel fronds, or dandelion petals. Serve right away for the best texture and taste.

Rose-Covered Fiddleheads with Burrata

Serves 3 to 4

3 cups fiddleheads, rinsed

Salt and freshly ground black pepper

Extra-virgin olive oil

2 to 3 (4-ounce) balls burrata, halved

2 tablespoons dried rose petals and fresh violets

Every spring, Maine literally sprouts the loveliest little green treats known as fiddleheads. Fiddleheads are the unfurled part of the ostrich fern and are considered somewhat of a delicacy in the Northeast during spring. While I have never foraged them for myself, fiddleheads are easy to find at stores all around Maine in the months of May and early June. You gotta act fast with these guys, as they grace us with their presence for such a short amount of time.

I like to keep it simple with fiddleheads, but you can always add them to pasta or salads or coat them in batter and give them a good deep fry. Always make sure you boil fiddleheads for a few minutes to make sure they are tender and easy to consume. This particular dish is meant to highlight the fiddleheads and not overpower them with an abundance of flavors.

Start by warming a medium saucepan of water over medium-high heat. Add a heavy pinch of salt as the water heats up. Once the water has come to a roaring boil, add the fiddleheads and set a timer for 5 minutes. Be careful not to overcook; they should be bright green and easy to pierce with a fork when they're done.

Once done, drain the fiddleheads and transfer them to a large serving plate. Drizzle with olive oil and season with salt and pepper to taste. Gently mix on the plate with clean hands to distribute the seasoning and oil.

Top the fiddleheads with the burrata, rose petals, and violets. Serve immediately or within a few hours. Store any leftovers covered in the fridge and consume within 3 days.

Fiddlehead Facts

+ Do not consume raw or undercooked fiddleheads.
This can lead to abdominal pain, upset stomach, and nausea.

+ You don't want to over boil your fiddleheads, so don't let them go for longer than 6 minutes.
You'll notice that the fiddleheads turn bright green when they are done.

+ Clean your fiddleheads! You can do this by soaking them for 10 minutes,
then giving them a good rinse. You want the brown papery stuff to come off.

+ You may notice that the ends of the fiddleheads start to brown after a few days in the fridge.
You can easily snap these ends off before cooking or slice them off with a paring knife.

Buttery Turmeric Baked Eggs

Serves 5 to 6

10 eggs

½ cup unsalted butter, thickly sliced

1 heaping tablespoon dried turmeric powder

½ tablespoon freshly ground black pepper

¼ teaspoon ground cinnamon

Salt

½ cup shredded Gruyère

½ cup shredded Asiago

Finely chopped fresh herbs (such as dill or basil), for garnish

If you're ever looking for easy breakfast food for a group of friends, this is your best bet. It's creamy, satisfying, and so damn delicious. The turmeric gives it a unique flavor and can help fight any inflammation you may have going on. Turmeric needs black pepper or fat to bind with in order to get its full medicinal value, so the mix of pepper and butter is perfect. Top these eggs with a mix of fresh herbs and hot sauce and serve alongside Perfect Roasted Potatoes (page 127) or Roasted Asparagus with Chamomile and Ghee (page 66).

+ + +

Preheat the oven to 350°F. Lightly grease a large 9 by 13-inch baking dish with oil or butter. Carefully crack the eggs into the prepared dish, taking care not to break any yolks. Place the butter slices in the baking dish with the eggs. Sprinkle the turmeric, pepper, cinnamon, and salt over the eggs, then scatter the cheese on top. Place the pan in the oven and cook for 8 to 10 minutes, until the eggs are cooked properly and to your liking. Cut the eggs into squares, top with the fresh herbs, and serve warm.

Herbed Sour Cream

Makes 1½ cups

1½ cups full-fat sour cream

2 tablespoons minced fresh dill

2 tablespoons minced fresh basil

1 tablespoon minced tulsi, fresh or dried

¼ teaspoon smoked paprika

¼ teaspoon chili powder

1 tablespoon minced garlic

Salt and freshly ground black pepper

Sour cream is my kryptonite. On a good week, our household (aka me) will go through a small container of the stuff because I am, to put it lightly, addicted to it. Sour cream goes with anything if you ask me. I'm a sucker for all food creamy, and sour cream makes that happen for me. Shell out the big bucks for the good heavy stuff or buy whatever is on sale. Sour cream is perfect for almost everything savory or sweet. Keep this stocked in your fridge and dollop on whatever you please. I like it best with Perfect Roasted Potatoes (page 127) or twenty-nine-cent packaged ramen.

✦ ✦ ✦

Place the sour cream, dill, basil, tulsi, paprika, chili powder, and garlic in a small bowl and combine well. Season with salt and pepper to taste. Serve right away or store in an airtight container in the fridge for up to 4 days. It's best served cold.

Witchy Bliss Balls

Makes 14 to 16 balls

Balls

2 cups rolled oats

4 tablespoons nut
or seed butter

½ cup maple syrup

1 teaspoon coconut oil

½ teaspoon ground ginger

1 teaspoon adaptogenic
powder

¼ teaspoon salt

¼ teaspoon ground
cardamom

¼ teaspoon ground
nutmeg

¼ teaspoon vanilla extract

Coating

1 tablespoon chia seeds

¼ cup shredded coconut

1 tablespoon dried
calendula petals
or rose petals

This is my version of Rosemary Gladstar's classic Zoom Balls, which is a recipe staple in the herbal community. The best thing about these little herbal balls is that you can pretty much add whatever you want or have on hand. As long as they stick together, you've got yourself a power-packed snack. Use any sort of nut or seed butter you like. I prefer sunflower seed butter for this recipe, as the taste is not too overpowering. Take these balls on hikes or long road trips or wrap them in a freezer-safe container and freeze for up to 1 month for later use.

+ + +

To make the balls, place all the ingredients in a food processor. Pulse until well combined and sticky enough to form a ball. Add more maple syrup, ½ teaspoon at a time, if the mixture isn't sticky enough to hold together. Before forming, taste and see whether you need to adjust any of the ingredients.

To make the coating, mix all the ingredients in a separate medium-size bowl. Form your oat mixture into 1-inch balls and then roll them into the coating. Line a baking sheet with parchment. Place the balls on the baking sheet. Continue with the remaining dough and coating. Store the balls in an airtight container in the fridge for up to 2 weeks.

Lavender-Matcha Iced Latte

Serves 1

1 cup milk, your choice

1 teaspoon matcha

1 teaspoon vanilla extract

1 to 2 teaspoons
Lavender Simple Syrup
(page 85)

Ice cubes

When my mom and I first moved to Chicago, I somehow ended up at an all-girls Catholic school deep on the southwest side of the city. During the two months I attended this institution, the most memorable things were the green tea frappuccinos combined with the manicures my mom would treat us to weekly. As Mainers in the big city in 2005, Starbucks was still a novelty to us, and we frequented the place as much as possible, on every corner possible. I've always struggled with traditional schooling, but this foreign Catholic school felt beyond anything I had experienced in my sixteen years. I found myself landing in detention more often than I'd like to admit. It felt like they doled them out like candy there! The after-school treats on the long drive back to our apartment in Hyde Park were a relief. I got my love of luxury from my mom, and this short stretch of weekly manicures was indeed luxurious. We got to sit in air-conditioning and faux leather chairs while sipping our drinks and getting our nails painted. Me, a prim little French tip, and my mother, undoubtedly some shade of pink.

It took me a while to realize that the green tea frappuccino from Starbucks was just a very American take on classic Japanese matcha tea. Once I figured this out, my appreciation of matcha grew, and I could not be stopped. All I thought about was matcha, and I hunted down every variation that I could find. Use whatever milk you like best to make this with. If you don't have a handheld frother, you can froth the milk and matcha by placing it in a quart-sized mason jar, capping it tightly, and shaking for about 1 minute, or until the milk is nice and frothy.

+ + +

Place the milk, matcha, and vanilla into a quart-sized mason jar. Using a handheld frother, mix together until frothy. Add the simple syrup to the milk. Add the desired amount of ice, pop in a straw, and drink cold.

Salty Sumac Cucumbers

Serves 1 to 2

1 large cucumber, peeled and sliced into ½-inch rounds

1½ tablespoons sumac

1 tablespoon extra-virgin olive oil

Salt and freshly ground black pepper

This snack was a staff favorite when I worked at an Ayurvedic bathhouse in Sebastopol, California. One of my coworkers would make a big bowl of it, and we'd all pass it around from room to room. Once spring hits, I stock my fridge with cucumbers and devour them daily. Try this when you need an easy cool-down snack as the days get warmer and you find yourself wanting to be indoors less and less.

Place all the ingredients in a large bowl and mix until the cucumbers are completely coated. Serve right away or cover and store in the fridge for up to 3 days.

About Sumac!

Sumac is a tart, lemony seasoning that is typically associated with Middle Eastern cuisine, though it is historically recorded in texts from around the world. Sumac is a versatile ingredient that can be used in both sweet and savory dishes. It's a cooling spice, which makes it ideal for warmer months. Although related, sumac spice is not to be confused with poisonous sumac.

Roasted Asparagus with Chamomile and Ghee

Serves 2 to 4

1 pound asparagus

1 tablespoon chamomile, fresh or dried

½ cup ghee

2 to 4 cloves garlic, minced

½ tablespoon honey

Salt and freshly ground black pepper

I love asparagus, but I feel like it's an easy vegetable to mess up. Like most food, the key is to make sure that it's properly seasoned and cooked the right amount of time. Undercooked or overcooked and not well-seasoned asparagus falls short of spectacular. This asparagus is full of flavor and cooked just enough that it sort of falls apart in your mouth. The chamomile adds a bright floral taste, while the honey tames any bitterness that the chamomile may contribute. It'll make you look at chamomile in a different way, because it isn't just your grandmother's bedtime tea after all.

Preheat the oven to 450°F. Wash the asparagus and cut the ends off where the stems fade to white. Place it in a baking dish (whatever size fits your spears) and add the remaining ingredients, making sure to coat the asparagus well. Bake for 10 minutes, then flip the asparagus using tongs. Bake for another 10 minutes, or until the tips have browned and you can easily puncture the asparagus with a fork. Transfer it to a serving dish and finish with more salt and pepper to taste. Serve warm or cold.

Herby-Honey Pizza Dough

Makes enough for 1 large pizza

1 tablespoon honey

¾ cup water, warm

2 cups all-purpose flour

1 packet instant yeast
(2¼ teaspoons)

1 heaping tablespoon
dried herb, your choice

1 teaspoon salt

1½ tablespoons extra-
virgin olive oil, plus
1 teaspoon, divided

Figuring out how to make pizza dough at home feels so powerful, and it's remarkably easy. I always like my crust a little on the sweet side, hence the honey. To me, there is nothing more delightful than pairing a flavorful crust with saucy, spicy toppings. Make this pizza dough ahead of time and keep it in the fridge for later use. You can also wrap the dough in a few layers of plastic wrap and keep it in the freezer for up to 2 months.

I suggest using nettles, thyme, or tulsi for the dried herbs in this crust, but any dried, flavorful herb will do!

Place the honey and water in a small bowl and mix until the honey has dissolved.

In a large bowl, add the flour, yeast, herb, and salt. Using a whisk, fluff the flour mixture for 1 minute, until everything is well combined. Add 1½ tablespoons of the olive oil and mix well, then pour in the water and honey mixture. Using a wooden spoon or your hands, mix the dough until shaggy in texture. Transfer the dough to a lightly floured surface and knead until smooth, then form the dough into a ball. Drizzle the remaining 1 teaspoon olive oil in the bowl, making sure to thoroughly coat it. Return the dough ball to the bowl, making sure to coat it with the olive oil in the bowl. Cover the bowl with a cloth and keep it in a warm spot. Once the dough has doubled in size, about 2 hours, punch it down and form it into a ball again. Use it right away or cover it in plastic wrap and keep it in the fridge for up to 1 week.

Dandelion Pesto Breakfast Pizza

Serves 4

Pesto

2 cups loosely packed chopped dandelion leaves

2 to 3 cloves garlic

½ cup extra-virgin olive oil

½ cup shredded Parmigiano-Reggiano cheese

1 cup sunflower seeds

Salt and freshly ground black pepper

Pizza

1 recipe Herby-Honey Pizza Dough (page 67)

4 teaspoons extra-virgin olive oil, divided

2 cups shredded Gouda cheese

½ large yellow or red onion, sliced into ½-inch strips

Salt and freshly ground black pepper

4 large eggs

Fennel fronds, calendula, and red pepper flakes, for garnish

When I was nineteen, I had a brief stint as a landscaper for a small company on Nantucket. I say brief because I was not cut out for landscaping like I had hoped I was. I'd give it my all in the morning, happily mulching or weeding in the shade, but by noon, I was slow as mud. I think the job lasted about a month before I was let go before work early one morning. Despite this being my first time getting fired and my general dislike of the job, I have really nice memories of getting coffee and small breakfast pizzas from a mid-island bakery before work. In my mind, I can still taste bites of cheesy bread, fresh herbs, and creamy egg that I washed down with hazelnut coffee. My love for those early morning pizzas will last forever, apparently. Cover with fresh herbs and serve warm or wrap them up in a towel or some parchment paper to take on the go. Make your own Herby-Honey Pizza Dough (page 67) or buy a premade one in the store.

+ + +

To make the pesto, place the dandelion leaves, garlic, olive oil, cheese, and sunflower seeds in a blender. Blend until combined and the pesto has a paste-like consistency. Add more olive oil (or even a teaspoon of water) to the pesto if the ingredients aren't breaking down properly. Taste and season to your liking with salt and pepper. The pesto will keep in an airtight jar in the fridge for up to 1 week.

To make the pizza, preheat the oven to 375°F. Using a bench scraper, divide the pizza dough into 4 quarters and roll 2 of them out until they are about ½ inch thick. Line two large baking sheets with parchment paper. Place two of the dough rounds on a baking sheet. Drizzle 1 teaspoon of the olive oil over each piece of dough, making sure to completely coat the dough with your hands or a brush. Next, add 1 heaping tablespoon pesto (or more if you'd like!) over each oiled dough, spreading it evenly. Top with Gouda, onion, and salt

and pepper, making sure to leave a little nest of cheese for the egg, which will be added later. Place the pizzas in the oven and cook for 5 minutes.

Remove the pan from the oven and carefully crack 1 egg into the middle of each pizza. Rotate the pan and return it to the oven, cooking for 20 more minutes. Once the egg has set and the dough is a crisp brown color, remove the pan from the oven. Top with a sprinkling of fennel fronds, calendula, and red pepper flakes.

Repeat the process with the remaining two pieces of dough and toppings. Serve straight away or cover with beeswax or plastic wrap and keep in the fridge for up to 4 days.

Summer

It's early summer now. Sherbet skies and lush grass make themselves known, once again signaling the start of long, warm days. As far as I know, this is the Montana that people seek when they move out here, the Montana they think of when their eyes light up as they speak of their elevated home under broad, beautiful skies.

Sharpened peaks jut into soft clouds, and the crickets sing merrily long into the night. The sun begins to set after 10 p.m., and you're in awe that it's this light so late. It feels good after being shell shocked by the short amount of daylight during the winter months. It's during June that I remember why I live here. Now that it's warm and the snow has melted on the pass to Idaho, we're finally able to get to our favorite hot springs. Though June is typically Montana's wet season, this season is already blistering hot. They say it'll break records this year. Regardless, we decide a soak is necessary. I pack my wicker suitcase with sunscreen, books, and knickknacks and toss it in the back seat of the truck. I'm wearing my new linen bloomers and a large sunhat. I look like a nineteenth-century beachgoer, and I am here for it.

The hot spring is about an hour and a half "up the road" from our cabin, and we set off after filling up on gas and Gatorade in town. The air smells like wood and honey, a true sign of Montana summer.

We head west along the highway, past forest service housing, roaming elk, and even a replica of a medieval castle that was built sometime in the '90s. We drive so far on this stretch of highway that the paved road turns to gravel and becomes so narrow that we have to pull over for oncoming traffic every now and then. As the truck climbs its way higher in elevation, I have Connor stop so I can get out and identify some familiar-looking plants. I snap pictures so I can properly identify them once we have cell service.

Once we get to the hot springs, we immediately go to the small hut that houses our favorite little pool. It's deep enough for both Connor and me to float comfortably, and the warmth of the water feels both invigorating and healing. We stay submerged for as long as our bodies can handle it, reading out loud the names of all the people who have stopped by here and engraved their names in the wood. We like to make up their stories and speculate whether the couples who have marked their names in pairs are still together all these years later. After about thirty minutes, we pull ourselves out of the spring and dry off, remarking on how magical this place is and how much we needed to come here.

We head back toward the truck and load up on cheese, crackers, and electrolytes. When we're full, we make our way to the creek to plunge our feet into the cold water. Connor catches a frog, and I play around with my new camera, snapping photos of burned trees and wildflowers. We smell of sulfur water and sunscreen, and we couldn't be happier. Montana winter can be hard and exhausting, but it's days like these in early summer that make it all worthwhile.

Honey Rose-Glazed Nectarine and Burrata Salad

Serves 2 to 4

½ cup honey

2 tablespoons balsamic vinegar

1 tablespoon rose water

1 heaping tablespoon dried rose petals

3 large ripe nectarines, washed, halved lengthwise, pits removed

2 to 3 (4-ounce) balls burrata

Salt and freshly ground black pepper

8 to 10 lemon balm leaves and dried rose petals

Oh, honey, the first time I made this, I fell in love at first bite. This is the perfect summer salad and a blend of all things creamy, sweet, and bright. This is the sort of dish I want to serve at a midsummer celebration with friends. It reminds me of summer twilight and white lacy dresses stained by fruit. It takes no more than twenty minutes to make and is ideal on hot summer days. If you don't have fresh lemon balm, add mint instead.

Preheat a grill pan or barbecue to medium-high heat. Place the honey, balsamic, rose water, and rose petals in a small bowl and whisk to combine.

Submerge the nectarines in the glaze one at a time, making sure to cover both sides.

Transfer the nectarines to the hot grill. Cook them for 2 minutes on each side, occasionally applying pressure with tongs, then transfer them to a cutting board. Repeat with any remaining nectarines. Cut the nectarine in half lengthwise again, re-submerge in the glaze, and return them to the grill. Cook each quarter for another 30 seconds on each side. Transfer them to a serving plate and top with the burrata, salt, pepper, lemon balm, and rose petals. Drizzle with any remaining glaze or more honey. Serve warm or cool.

Elderflower and Chamomile Midsommar Cake

Serves 8 to 10

Syrup
3 cups water

1½ cups cane sugar

1 cup chamomile

1 lemon, sliced

1½ cups elderflower

Cake
4 large eggs, separated

Pinch of salt

¾ cup cane sugar

1 tablespoon water

2 teaspoons vanilla extract

1 tablespoon baking powder

¾ cup all-purpose flour

Berry Mix
1 cup strawberries, stemmed, hulled, and cut into small pieces

½ cup raspberries

1 cup cane sugar

Frosting
8 tablespoons (1 stick) unsalted butter, softened

3 cups confectioners' sugar

1 teaspoon rosewater

Pinch of salt

¼ teaspoon vanilla extract

1½ tablespoons milk or cream

Toppings
1 to 2 cups fresh fruit

Lemon balm

Fresh mint

Simply put, this is a stunner of a cake. It's my take on a classic Swedish Midsommar cake, and it always brings me so much joy to not only eat but also look at. The first summer I spent in Sweden, Midsommar was the highlight of my first month there. My friends and I dressed up in our finest farmer threads, donned handmade flower crowns, drank too much aquavit, and ate a lot of pickled herring with eggs, dill, and potatoes (my personal favorite).

I was stunned at the beauty and whimsy of my first Midsommar in Sweden, so, for me, this cake represents that feeling. The berry mix reminds me of the wild ones we harvested in the forest just outside the farm and the tiny jordgubbar (strawberries) we plucked from gardens on our way to the lake. The elderflower and chamomile syrup is reminiscent of the elderflower saft we'd make in large buckets to sell in the café. This is a sweet juice concentrate, similar to a syrup, that has to be diluted with water. To this day, it is one of the best things I've ever tasted.

Brushing a flavored syrup on a cake before frosting it is a wonderful way to keep the cake moist and add a unique herbal flavor that will be certain to wow your guests. Serve this cake at any summer soirée or in the depths of winter when you need a cheerful pick-me-up. I like to eat mine with a glass of champagne and a shot of aquavit on the side.

+ + +

Start by making the syrup the day before you want to serve the cake. Place the water and sugar in a medium pot over medium-high heat. Once the water has boiled and the sugar has dissolved, remove the pot from heat and add the chamomile, lemon, and elderflower to the water. Stir and cover the pot with a lid. Infuse on the stovetop overnight. Strain the mixture, using a fine mesh strainer, into a quart-sized jar or appropriately sized bottle. Keep it in the fridge for up to 2 months.

To make the cake, preheat the oven to 350°F and line two 7-inch cake pans with parchment paper to prevent sticking.

Place the egg whites and salt in a medium bowl. Beat with an electric whisk for 6 to 8 minutes, until the egg whites form stiff peaks, then set aside.

In a separate medium bowl, mix the egg yolks, sugar, water, and vanilla with a whisk for about 5 minutes, or until the batter has become light and doubled in size. Gently fold in the egg whites, add the baking powder, then sprinkle in the flour, ¼ cup at a time.

Once mixed, pour the batter into the cake pans and place them in the oven. Bake for 15 to 18 minutes, until the tops are a golden color and the cake has set.

To make the berry mix, while the cakes are baking, combine the berries and sugar in a clean bowl. Set aside.

To make the frosting, combine the butter, confectioners' sugar, rose water, salt, vanilla, and milk in a large bowl. Using a hand mixer, beat until thick, adding more confectioners' sugar if needed to reach your desired consistency. Place it in the freezer or fridge to set and keep cool.

Once the cakes are done, let them cool completely before removing them from the pans. You don't want your cakes to be warm at all; otherwise, the frosting will melt off.

Using a pastry brush, slather the syrup onto the cakes (use ½ to ¾ cup total) and let sit for 10 minutes or so. Transfer one layer to a clean plate or cake stand and start frosting. Once the bottom layer is frosted, spread the berry mix evenly over the bottom layer. Place the second layer on top and use the remaining frosting to completely cover the cake. Pile on fresh fruit, lemon balm, mint, or whatever you fancy and serve.

Lilac Peachy Pops

Makes 4 to 6 popsicles

1 (13.5-ounce) can full-fat coconut milk

1 cup chopped peaches, peeled fresh or frozen

1 cup maple syrup

½ cup lilacs

Once you figure out how to make popsicles at home, there is no turning back. Having control over the ingredients you add to homemade popsicles is a life changer, and there are so many ways to do it. Freeze your favorite herbal tea mixed with coconut milk or yogurt or puree those on-the-brink strawberries and mix in some rose petals and rose water. No matter what you dream up, you'll find that these are the perfect refresher for hot summer evenings, and there's no cooking required! You can pick up a simple popsicle mold at almost any store in the summer months and always online, of course. The number of popsicles made with this recipe will vary by the size of the mold, so keep that in mind.

Place the coconut milk, peaches, and maple syrup in a blender and mix until smooth and well combined. Add the lilacs to the blender jar and fold them in with a spatula until they are distributed throughout the mixture. Pour the mixture into the popsicle molds and keep them in the freezer for at least 2 hours, or until the popsicles slide out with ease.

Shatavari Kale Caesar Salad

Serves 4 to 5

4 cups kale, stemmed and chopped or torn small

1 teaspoon extra-virgin olive oil or coconut oil

Dressing

3 to 5 anchovy fillets

2 cloves garlic

1 large egg yolk

1 teaspoon fresh lemon juice

1 teaspoon shatavari

1 tablespoon Dijon mustard

½ teaspoon Worcestershire sauce

½ cup grapeseed or sunflower oil

¼ cup grated Parmesan, plus more for serving

Salt and freshly ground black pepper

Herbed Croutons (page 125)

There is no salad I love more than the classic Caesar salad. I'll take it plain or with chicken or a grilled portabella. Either way, I almost always want a Caesar salad. Finding a good one, however, can be tricky. I didn't start making my own from scratch until recently.

I like to use kale for my salads since it can be hard to find good romaine lettuce year round in Montana. Plus, kale feels a little more hearty. Just make sure you give your kale a good massage and remove the leaf from the stem. I like to tear my kale rather than chop it. Top with the Herbed Croutons (page 125) or the Crispy Tulsi Chickpeas (page 138). I personally never say no to an anchovy. This recipe contains a raw egg yolk, which is fine to consume every now and then!

+ + +

Place the chopped or torn kale in a large bowl. Drizzle the oil over the kale and, using your hands, massage the kale for 1 to 2 minutes. Set it aside and let it rest while you make the dressing.

To make the dressing, place the anchovy fillets in a separate large salad bowl. Using a fork, mash the fillets into a fine paste. Using a Microplane zester, grate the garlic cloves into the bowl with the anchovies. Add the egg yolk, lemon juice, shatavari, Dijon, and Worcestershire to the bowl. Using a handheld whisk, mix until smooth and well combined. Slowly add the oil while whisking continuously. (You can place a tea towel under the bowl to help it stay in place if needed.) Once the oil is combined, fold in the Parmesan and season with salt and pepper to taste.

Transfer the kale to the salad bowl with the dressing and toss to coat the kale. Cover with croutons and a desired amount of additional Parmesan. Serve right away.

Peach-Rooibos Sun Tea

Makes 1 gallon

1 cup loose-leaf rooibos tea

1 lemon, sliced

2 cups peaches, sliced, skin on

1 cup cane sugar or honey

1 gallon water

The first coffee shop I worked at was called the Bean. Located right in the heart of town on Nantucket, the Bean was the go-to hangout for my friends, and working there became a rite of passage in a way. You'd often be able to find one of us sitting outside on one of the green benches, inside working behind the counter, or bantering with one of the locals. The Bean felt like home, with its wide windows, creaky floors, worn seats, and wall of jars filled with tea. This tea wall was, in my mind, the showstopper of the place. You could find almost any tea imaginable, and it became my library as I began my foray into herbalism. My favorite tea, however, was the peach rooibos. A blend of creamy red rooibos and bits of dried peach, this tea was perfection to me and, undoubtedly, one of our bestsellers. Making a sun tea version of that blend is perfect for summer—comforting, cooling, and so easy to make. You'll be sipping this sweet(ish) tea all summer long. Skip the sugar if you prefer unsweetened tea.

Place the tea in a cotton drawstring tea bag or strip of cheesecloth. Tie tightly and add to a gallon-sized jar or decanter, along with the lemons, peaches, and sugar. Cover with water and place the jar in a sunny spot outside. Keep it in the sun all day, or for at least 4 hours, and stir occasionally. Place in the fridge before nightfall and serve cold. The tea will keep in the fridge for up to 1 week.

Herbal Simple Syrups

Knowing how to make a good herbal simple syrup will level up your cocktail, mocktail, and iced coffee game. And they are truly as simple to make as the name implies. Each of the following recipes represents different types of herbs and how to make syrups with them. One has dried delicate flowers, one has fresh herbs, one is potent, and one is a root.

Rose Simple Syrup

Makes 2 cups

2 cups water

1 cup cane sugar

1 cup dried rose petals

Boiling flowers can damage the flavor and the essential oil that all plants possess. I add the roses to hot (not boiling water) and let the petals infuse slowly and the sugar dissolve. This recipe works with other flowers and dried herbs such as calendula, chamomile, tulsi, etc.

Place the water and sugar in a small pot over medium-high heat, stirring so that the sugar dissolves as it heats. Once the water has come to a gentle simmer, remove the pot from the heat and add the rose petals. Stir, cover the pot, and infuse overnight.

Using a finely woven handheld strainer, strain the liquid into a quart-sized jar. Cap it tightly and keep it in the fridge for up to 6 weeks.

Sage Simple Syrup

Makes 2 cups

2 cups water

1 cup cane sugar

½ cup tightly packed fresh culinary sage

This syrup reminds me of harvesting sage and other culinary herbs from the garden behind Oldest House on Nantucket, where I first started learning about herbalism. Whenever I am back on the island, I head to the garden to harvest some sage and rosemary to bring back to Montana, where I dry the herbs and burn them in a seashell whenever I'm feeling homesick. Sage is easy to grow in pots. This syrup goes well in tea, soda water, or the Sage Margarita on page 164.

Place the water and sugar in a small pot over medium-high heat, stirring so that the sugar dissolves as it heats. Once the water has come to a gentle simmer, remove the pot from the heat and add the sage. Stir, cover the pot, and infuse overnight. Using a finely woven handheld strainer, strain the liquid into a quart-sized jar. Cap tightly and keep in the fridge for up to 6 weeks.

Lavender Simple Syrup

Makes 2 cups

2 cups water

1 cup honey

¼ cup dried lavender

This lavender syrup is the perfect example of taking a bitter herb and making it sweet. Use less of the herb if it's very potent so the flavor doesn't overpower your syrup (rosemary, cinnamon, and mugwort are other examples). Pair with the Lavender-Matcha Latte (page 64). Honey can replace the sugar in any of these recipes.

+ + +

Place the water in a small pot over medium-high heat. Once the water has come to a gentle simmer, remove the pot from the heat and add the lavender and honey. Stir until the honey has dissolved. Cover the pot and infuse for 1 to 2 hours.

Using a finely woven handheld strainer, strain the liquid into a quart-sized jar. Cap it tightly and keep it in the fridge for up to 6 weeks.

Burdock-Ginger Simple Syrup

Makes 2 cups

2 cups water

¾ cup dried burdock

½ cup ginger, peeled and coarsely chopped

1 cup cane sugar

The flavor of this syrup packs an earthy, pungent punch, what herbalists call a "medicinal flavor." Make sure to boil the roots for twenty minutes to extract the medicinal benefits. If you like the classic Maine soda Moxie, then this syrup is for you. Add it to soda water or chai or brush on top of a cake!

+ + +

Place the water in a medium pot and bring to a boil over medium-high heat. Add the burdock and ginger to the boiling water and boil for 20 minutes, until the water is a deep brown color. Remove the pot from the heat and add the sugar, stirring until the sugar has dissolved. Cover the pot and infuse for 1 to 2 hours.

Using a finely woven handheld strainer, strain the liquid into a clean quart-sized jar. Cap it tightly and keep it in the fridge for up to 6 weeks.

Buttered Radishes with Herbal Gomasio

Serves 4 to 6

Herbal Gomashio

¼ cup sesame seeds

¼ cup dried nettles

¼ cup milk thistle seeds

2 tablespoons dried calendula

1 tablespoon kombu flakes

2 to 3 tablespoons kosher salt, depending on taste

Radishes

1 bunch radishes, leaves and stems intact, washed and dried

1 cup (2 sticks) salted butter

Radishes seem to be one of those often overlooked vegetables. Until a few years ago, I wasn't aware of their potential and viewed them as a garnish or an unnecessary addition to a perfectly good salad. I was so wrong! Radishes, when given proper attention, are just stunning and a great standalone snack. This is a classically French dish with a flavorful twist. Gomashio, which translates to "sesame salt," is a Japanese seasoning that is often kept on tabletops and used to top rice, soups, salads, or anything else your sweetheart desires. Plus, it makes a great salt substitute. Just reduce the amount of salt used and add more kombu for that salty flavor.

Serve these radishes with some rosé and a good group of friends. The better the butter, the better this snack will be. So if there is ever a time to treat yourself to some supremely delicious yellow butter, it's now.

✦ ✦ ✦

To make the gomashio, place the sesame seeds in a small pan over medium heat. Gently stir the seeds until they are lightly browned. Once toasted, place the sesame seeds in a food processor, along with the remaining ingredients. Pulse until the ingredients have become broken down into small bits and well combined. Taste and add more salt or other ingredients as needed. Store the gomashio in a jar with a lid and keep with your spices. It will keep on your countertop for up to 6 months.

To make the radishes, melt the butter in a small pan over medium-low heat for 3 to 4 minutes, or in your microwave using a heat-safe bowl for 45 seconds to 1 minute. You want the butter to be thick yet runny, sort of resembling custard. Once the butter has melted, hold a radish by the stem and dip it in the butter. Set the radish on a large plate or tray. Repeat the process with all radishes. While the butter on the radishes is still warm, sprinkle on the desired amount of gomashio. Once done, place them in the fridge to allow the butter to set. Serve at room temperature.

Harriet's Tomato and Herby Mayo Sandwich

Makes 2 to 3 sandwiches

Herby Mayo

1 cup mayonnaise

1 teaspoon thyme

2 tablespoons dill, chopped

¼ teaspoon smoked paprika

½ teaspoon red pepper flakes

1 teaspoon minced garlic

Salt and freshly ground black pepper

Sandwich

4 to 6 slices of bread, your choice

1 large heirloom tomato, washed and cut into ½-inch slices

Salt

I credit Harriet the Spy with all my writer tendencies and dreams. I was obsessed with the movie for years and even renamed myself Harriet for an entire summer (complete with the yellow raincoat and composition notebook). One of the most memorable things from the book and movie is Harriet's favorite meal, the tomato sandwich. The same summer I renamed myself, my family made sure to pack tomato sandwiches for my daily camp lunch. After a good swim at the beach, I'd often dig a little hole in the sand, cover myself with a towel, and unwrap my sandwich with great care. This cemented my love for salty air, coziness, and hiding from the sun while enjoying a comforting little meal.

Use any fresh or dried herb you have on hand. The herbs I list here are merely delicious guidelines. Bonus points if you cover the sandwich with plastic wrap, let it get soggy, and eat it on a beach somewhere.

PS. Always, always, always salt your tomatoes! Salt enhances the flavor and is an important part of tomato consumption. Kosher or flakey salt is ideal, but use whatever you have in your cupboard.

+ + +

To make the herby mayo, place all the ingredients in a small bowl and mix well. To make the sandwich, slather each side of the bread with your desired amount of mayo. Top each slice of bread with tomato, finish with some salt, and top with another piece of bread, if desired. This makes a perfect open-faced or classic sandwich. You'll most definitely have extra mayo, so store it in your fridge for up to 1 week.

Ricotta-Stuffed Nasturtium Flowers

Serves 15 to 18

2 tablespoons oil or unsalted butter

1 large yellow onion, chopped small

1 tablespoon fresh thyme, or ½ tablespoon dried thyme

Salt and freshly ground black pepper

1 tablespoon honey

1 clove black garlic, crushed

2 cups ricotta cheese

15 to 18 nasturtium flowers

Nasturtium flowers are a hidden gem of the flower world. Not only can you find them in many gardens but also they are absolutely delicious. Nasturtium flowers have a very peppery, almost spicy flavor, which makes them perfect for savory dishes. These stuffed flowers are perfect for any summer day and look pretty darn good on a plate. Make the stuffing ahead of time and pick the nasturtiums as needed. I've had the worst luck growing them, but maybe you will have better luck than me. If not, reach out to your best gardening buddy and see whether they have any or check out your local farmers' market. If I'm in the mood for a little spice, I'll add a tablespoon of sambal or some red pepper flakes to the ricotta mix.

Place the oil in a heavy-bottom pan over medium-high heat. When the oil is hot, add the onions and season with the thyme, salt, and pepper, honey, and garlic. Cook for 10 minutes, until the onions are translucent. Remove the pan from the heat and let the onions cool.

In a large bowl, add the onions and ricotta cheese and season with more salt and pepper if desired.

To stuff the flowers, first inspect them for any bugs or debris and remove as necessary. Add the ricotta-and-onion mixture 1 tablespoon at a time. Use your best judgment on how much you can fill each flower. Transfer the flowers to a serving plate, cover with plastic wrap, and place in the fridge to keep the flowers from wilting before serving. You can make these up to 3 hours before serving. They are best consumed the same day.

Minty Lemon Balm–Coconut Rice

Serves 2

1 cup jasmine rice, washed

1 cup canned full-fat coconut milk

1 cup water

¼ cup fresh or dried lemon balm

¼ cup fresh mint leaves

1 tablespoon honey

I could eat rice almost every day of the week. Coconut rice has long been made in regions of Africa, Asia, and the Caribbean, as that is where coconuts, and most rice, are native. This is my take on a dish that I find so comforting and versatile. Pair it with a protein or roasted veggies. Boil the leftovers with more coconut milk to make a creamy porridge. I made this in my rice cooker, which is a lifesaver for me, but you can always make it on your stovetop. If using dried lemon balm, make sure to add it about halfway through the cooking process to extract the flavor and soften the herb.

To wash your rice: Add dried rice to a bowl and cover with water. Rinse once, then cover with water again. Keep rinsing the rice until the water runs clear and not cloudy.

+ + +

Place the rice, coconut milk, and water in a rice cooker or medium pot. Cook according to the directions on the package. Once the rice is done, add the lemon balm, mint, and honey to the pot. Stir well and serve warm.

Rose Water Pomegranate with Yogurt

Serves 1 to 2

1 cup pomegranate seeds

1 teaspoon food-grade rose water

1 cup yogurt

Agave or honey

Mint leaves and rose petals, for garnish

*One of my favorite herb school teachers, Trinity Ava, introduced me to this snack. Trinity is a force of a woman, and I absolutely loved her approach to herbalism. I credit Trinity with my no-nonsense attitude toward essential oils (like, please **do not** consume essential oils!) and my love of adding in herbal goodness anywhere you can. During class one day, Trinity broke open a pomegranate and tossed it into a bowl with some rose water. She passed the bowl around as if it were popcorn. I hadn't had anything like it at that point, and it was a total dream to me. Adding yogurt makes it the perfect breakfast or even a dessert. Double the recipe and plate it on a large serving platter for gatherings.*

✦ ✦ ✦

Place the pomegranate seeds and rose water in a small bowl and toss. Spread the yogurt over a medium plate and cover with the pomegranate seeds. Drizzle the agave over the seeds to your desired taste. Garnish with fresh mint leaves, rose petals, and serve.

Garlicky Tomato Galette with Herbed Crust and Chèvre

Serves 2 to 4

1 pound heirloom tomatoes, cut into ½-inch slices

½ small red onion, thinly sliced

3 to 4 cloves garlic, minced

1 teaspoon dried lemon balm

1 teaspoon fresh thyme, or ½ teaspoon dried thyme

1 teaspoon fresh oregano, or ½ teaspoon dried oregano

Salt and freshly ground black pepper

1 recipe the Only Pie Crust (page 172)

1 (4-ounce) log chèvre, crumbled, divided

A Good Egg Wash (page 173)

Fresh basil leaves

Rumor has it that my mom voraciously craved tomatoes throughout her pregnancy with me. So I guess you can say that I've been a massive fan of the little fruits since conception. The smell of fresh tomato plants takes me back to my days at Rosenhill. I'd spend hours in the greenhouse, pruning the plants, counting down the days till harvest, when I could pluck the hot tomatoes straight from the vine and slice them up in the kitchen just a hundred yards away. In my opinion, there's nothing better than a warm tomato, sprinkled with herbs and a healthy helping of flakey salt. If it were reasonable to survive off of tomatoes, cheese, and a little bit of oil, you know I would. The crust for this galette is the same as the pie crust on page 172, but with herbs! The instructions for the herby crust are fully laid out here for you.

+ + +

Preheat the oven to 350°F. Place the tomato slices on a large tea towel or layer of paper towels and let sit for 10 minutes in order to remove some of the liquid. Transfer the tomato slices to a large bowl. Add the onions, garlic, lemon balm, thyme, and oregano. Season with salt and pepper to your liking. Mix well.

Line a baking sheet with parchment paper. Roll out the dough into an 12-inch circle that's ½ inch thick, then transfer it to the baking sheet. Sprinkle half the chèvre onto the rolled-out dough, then place the tomato mixture over the chèvre, leaving at least 1 inch of space between the filling and the edge of the dough.

Fold the dough edges over the filling, then brush the dough with egg wash. Sprinkle the remaining cheese on top and bake for 35 to 45 minutes, until the crust has browned. Remove the baking sheet from the oven. Serve the galette warm or cold with fresh basil leaves on top. It will keep in the fridge for 3 days.

Compound Butter

Compound butter is one of the easier things to make yet still looks and feels so very fancy. You can make compound butter sweet or savory, slather it on anything you like, or use it in place of regular butter in cooking or baking. When making compound butter, always start with unsalted butter so you have control over how much salt goes in the mix. Butter will keep in the fridge for up to one month. You can also freeze compound butter for up to three months. Freezing compound butter is a great way to prolong use and enjoy a summer herb or foraged mushroom in colder months.

Chanterelle Mushroom and Sage Butter

Makes 1½ cups

1 tablespoon unsalted butter, plus 1 cup, at room temperature, divided

½ cup chanterelle mushrooms

¼ teaspoon Chinese Five Spice

1 pinch red pepper flakes

Salt and freshly ground black pepper

6 to 8 fresh sage leaves

This recipe calls for chanterelle mushrooms, but you can use portobello, lion's mane, chicken of the woods, or whatever mushrooms you have on hand.

+ + +

Place 1 tablespoon of the butter in a small skillet over medium heat. Once the butter has melted, add the mushrooms. Sauté the mushrooms and season them with the Chinese Five Spice, red pepper flakes, and salt. Once the mushrooms have browned, remove the skillet from the heat and let cool.

Cut the mushrooms and sage into small pieces using a knife.

In a small bowl, mash the remaining 1 cup butter with a fork. Season accordingly with salt and pepper. Add the mushrooms and sage and mix. Transfer the butter to a sheet of wax paper and form into your desired shape. Wrap it well and place it in the fridge to harden. The butter will keep for up to 1 month.

Rose Petal, Brown Sugar, and Calendula Cocoa Butter

Makes 1½ cups

1 cup unsalted butter, at room temperature

2 tablespoons dried rose petals

2 tablespoons calendula petals

2 tablespoons brown sugar

1 teaspoon cocoa powder

¼ teaspoon ground cinnamon

¼ teaspoon ground cardamom

Pinch of flakey salt

Place the butter in a small bowl and mash with a fork. Next, add the remaining ingredients, reserving the salt for later, and mix. Once combined, add the salt one pinch at a time until you are happy with the taste. Transfer the butter to a sheet of wax paper and form into your desired shape. Wrap it well and place it in the fridge to harden. The butter will keep for 1 month.

Other combinations:

Start with at least 1 cup of unsalted butter and follow your own taste preference for these combinations. I'm hoping that you will use your own kitchen intuition for the ingredients. Over the years I've learned so much about cooking, but one of the most valuable things I've learned is how to follow my own personal flavor preference. Use the previous recipes as a guide for the ones that follow. Listen to your own taste buds and add or subtract as you see fit.

+ Edible flowers and poached pear

+ Cayenne, rosemary, and caramelized onion

+ Tulsi and basil

+ Nettle, smoky paprika, and roasted garlic

+ Turmeric, black pepper, and cardamom

Spencre and the Rose: A Love Story

There was a time in herb school where I had an "addiction" to rose petals. I put them in everything I ate, from stir-fries to creamy cashew pasta and tacos. I carried a small plastic bag of petals with me wherever I went, topping my food or drinks with them. I couldn't be stopped. It concerned me enough that I pulled one of my teachers aside and asked whether there was something wrong with me and whether I should put a stop to my wild behavior. She told me that she went through something similar with another herb when she was younger and it happens to the best of us. I can't remember what made me cool my jets with the rose intake, but I did slow down eventually.

Rose is one of those plants that I've been enamored with for most of my life. Not just the ones you buy from the store, but the wild roses that grow along many of the Nantucket beaches. I remember collecting rose petals and trying to make perfume with them by sticking the petals in a jar of water and leaving it on my windowsill. After a few days, it was the vilest-smelling concoction, but I was a little witch who wanted to try it all. The smell couldn't deter me from trying again.

In traditional Chinese medicine, rose is considered to be Shen tonic, which means that it is a medicine that directly aids and nourishes the spirit or emotional heart. Rose is considered a plant to gladden the heart, lift one's mood, and calm the nerves. So perhaps my short-term addiction to rose was the plant calling me in to heal my own wounded heart and spirit. I believe that plants can speak to us in this way and that my voracious craving was rose finding its way to me. Listen to these herbal cravings. Most likely, there is a good reason your body is wanting to consume the herb that is on your mind. I needed the heart-healing ways of rose as I navigated my way through the grief and stuck trauma I was rehashing during that time. I often joked that my time at herb school was just one long therapy camp, and I can thank the herbs for the healing that took place then.

Rhubarb, Strawberry, Plum, Rose Sauce

Makes about 3 cups

1 cup rhubarb, peeled and chopped

2 cups strawberries, stemmed, hulled, and chopped

2 cups plums, pitted and chopped

½ teaspoon ground cinnamon

2 tablespoons rose water

1 cup cane sugar

½ cup dried rose petals

This is my version of summer in a jar. It's got all our summertime besties: roses, plums, and, of course, rhubarb. Use this sauce on top of ice cream or crackers and cheese or smear it on toast with some mascarpone. This is simple to make and so rewarding to eat.

Place the rhubarb, strawberries, plums, cinnamon, rose water, and sugar in a large heavy-bottomed pan over medium heat. Cook for 8 to 10 minutes, until the fruit has broken down and the sugar has dissolved. Add the rose petals and turn the heat to low. Continue to cook until you can drag a spoon through the sauce and leave a clean trail on the bottom of the pan. Remove the pan from the heat, let the mixture cool, and transfer it to a clean quart-sized jar. This will keep in the fridge for up to 2 weeks.

Crispy-Crunchy Cumin Oil

Makes 1½ cups

1½ cups vegetable or peanut oil

4 large shallots, thinly sliced

2 cinnamon sticks

1 head garlic, peeled and thinly sliced

1 to 2 dried cayenne peppers, crushed

1 tablespoon cumin seeds

6 cardamom pods, crushed

¼ cup red pepper flakes

1 tablespoon brown sugar

2 tablespoons soy sauce

I love a good sauce. There's truly nothing more delightful to me than layering flavors and making everything as spicy as I can handle. This oil is a fantastic burst of flavor that's perfect for adding to toast, pizza, roasted veggies, or fish . . . really anything your heart desires. Sure, you can buy something similar, but it's pretty simple to make at home, and then you have complete control over the ingredient list, which is always a win in my book. Crush the cardamom pods and cayenne peppers using a mortar and pestle or the flat side of a blade.

Place the oil in a large pot over medium-low heat and warm for about 5 minutes, or until hot. Add the shallots, cinnamon sticks, garlic, and cayenne peppers and cook for 25 to 30 minutes, until the shallots and garlic have browned.

While the oil is cooking, in a large bowl combine the cumin, cardamom pods, red pepper flakes, brown sugar, and soy sauce and mix well. Using a handheld strainer, strain the oil into the bowl with the spices and sugar. Remove the cinnamon sticks and set the garlic, pepper, and shallots aside to cool. Mix the oil and spices together. Once the shallots and garlic have completely cooled, return them to the oil. Store the oil in an airtight jar on the countertop for 1 month.

Strawberry-Rose Bud Lemonade

Makes 5 cups

1 cup strawberries, hulled and chopped

¼ cup cane sugar

1 cup Rose Simple Syrup (page 84)

1½ cups freshly squeezed lemon juice (about 7 to 8 lemons)

4 to 5 cups cold water

Nothing says summer quite like lemonade. Add roses and strawberries to that and you're in paradise. For sake of simplicity and year-round enjoyment, the roses I used for the syrup in this recipe are dried. If you do use fresh, double the amount of rose petals. You can find the recipe for Rose Simple Syrup on page 84. Make sure you don't use store-bought roses with the intention of consuming them. Most store-bought roses are sprayed with pesticides, and no one wants that in their glass at a party. Juice your own lemons or buy store-bought lemon juice; there's no judgment here!

Place the strawberries and sugar in a large pitcher and muddle for 2 to 3 minutes, until the strawberries have broken down. Add the rose syrup, lemon juice, and 4 cups of water. Stir well and taste, adding the last cup of water if needed. Keep this in the fridge for up to 3 days. Serve cold.

Crispy Lemon Balm Leaves

Serves 2 to 4

About 1 cup fresh lemon balm leaves

½ cup oil

Salt

Whenever you need a good crunch for your meal, these crispy lemon balm leaves are here to help you out. They are perfect on top of a creamy pasta dish, baked goods, or even a smoky cocktail. This would also be wonderful with culinary sage leaves.

+ + +

Place the oil in a small pan over high heat and carefully drop the leaves in a few at a time. Fry them for only a second or two before removing them with tongs. Line a plate with paper towels and place them on the plate. Repeat this step with all the leaves. Top the fried leaves with a bit of salt and let cool.

Lemon Balm Mojito

Makes 1 drink

5 lemon balm leaves

3 mint leaves

1 teaspoon cane sugar

½ lime, cut into wedges

2 ounces white rum

Ice cubes

2 to 3 ounces club soda

Fresh mint or lemon balm sprigs, for garnish

Lime wedge, for garnish

Mojitos were my gateway cocktail (unless you count Shirley Temples at age five). At sixteen years old, my friends and I thought we were grown-ass adults and would frequent Lola 41, the hot new restaurant next to my house, on a weekly basis. We'd order virgin mojitos, overpriced sparkling water, and the occasional sushi roll and undoubtedly undertip our server. Virgin mojitos became the drink of the summer. I loved them so much that I carried around a tin of mojito-flavored mints, popping them frequently and making a big show of the tin so people would think I was trendy and sophisticated in my Old Navy flip-flops and worn-out flare jeans. This is a grown-up herby version of my beloved drink and bound to keep you feeling fancy all summer long.

Place the lemon balm, mint, sugar, and limes in a cocktail mixer and muddle for about 15 seconds. Add the rum and ice cubes and shake well. Strain into a tall glass and top with club soda. Garnish with mint or lemon balm sprigs and a lime wedge.

The Homestead

Montana

It takes forty-five minutes and two gates to get to the homestead from the main road. The gravel path is full of deep ruts and steep hills that require four-wheel drive and a decent clearance to get to our destination. Depending on the time of year, the road to the homestead is surrounded by purple and bright pink wildflowers or sage brush that smells so strong and sweet it permeates the cab of our little Ford Ranger. My favorite days are the rarest in this part of Montana: the days in June when fog hangs heavy over the green grass and the air is chilled and fresh as snowmelt.

We can access the homestead for only about six months because of the amount of snow throughout most of the year. The elevation in this part of Montana is about 5,000 feet, which isn't much in the grand scheme of things, but it's enough to keep the back roads covered in thick drifts of snow. When Connor and I are finally able to get up to the homestead in late May or early June, we are almost giddy with excitement on the ride up. This homestead has been in Connor's family since 1922. His great-grandfather, William, acquired the land in the Homestead Act, and, for the most part, it has remained greatly untouched since then. There is no electricity or running water, and the cabin's main heat source is the heavy wood-burning stove Connor's uncle built in '93 that sits in the middle of the room.

As soon as we arrive at the meadow that opens up to the cabin and the rest of the property, we take a left and head straight to the natural spring to collect some water before settling into the cabin. The spring is a simple spigot that juts out of the ground. There is no off switch or valve to shut it off, so mountain spring water runs wildly day and night. Horsetail, clovers, and nettles grow abundantly near the spring, and I make note of what I'd like to harvest. It's nothing short of magic and the best water I've ever consumed. Some days, we take our clothes off and let the water run over our backs, faces, and feet, relishing in the renewal and freshness as though it's our own sort of baptism, signifying a new season.

Once we are dry and stocked up on water, we bundle up and head back toward the little log cabin. We unload food, water, books, and our cats and assess the subtle changes made to the one-room cabin by Connor's uncle. Sometimes it's as simple as moving the food and coffee that expired in 1998 to a higher cabinet or as intricate as a beautiful new shelf made from the homestead's wood. Once we take our yearly cabin tour, we light a fire in the stove, set a pot of water over the heat, and drop in some coffee grounds. As we wait for it to boil, we get cozy and crack open a book or press play on our favorite podcast—pre-downloaded of course, because there's no cell service on the homestead. Since meeting Connor, this cabin ritual of ours has become almost sacred to me. This land is special and showed me that I can feel at home even in Montana, something that I didn't think possible until Connor brought me up here after a year or so of dating. I always take time to thank the land for allowing me to feel so at home, because in a world like this, with so many places to land, it feels pretty special to be able to land here.

Reishi Mushroom–Balsamic Reduction

Makes 1 cup

2 cups balsamic vinegar

6 to 8 slices dried reishi, broken in half

½ cup dark brown sugar

A good balsamic reduction is one of my favorite ways to add more flavor to my meals. When I learned how to make it at home, I was thrilled and shocked at how simple it is. You can use any sugar you'd like, but I use dark brown sugar for some depth. You can find dried reishi slices at your local herb shop or mushroom farm or online. I usually leave the reishi pieces in the balsamic reduction, but feel free to pick them out with little tongs or your fingers if you'd like. If you do leave them in, I don't suggest eating the mushroom pieces, as they are tough and not pleasant. Drizzle this reduction over the Roasted Root Salad (page 181) or the Garlicky Tomato Galette with Herbed Crust and Chèvre (page 94).

✦ ✦ ✦

Place all the ingredients in a medium pot over medium-high heat. Bring to a boil, then lower the heat to medium-low and simmer for 15 to 20 minutes. Once the vinegar has thickened and reduced by half, remove the pot from the heat and let the reduction cool, then transfer to a pint-sized jar. You can pick the reishi pieces out or leave them in. Keep this in the fridge for up to 1 month.

Herb-Infused Vinegars

Herbal vinegars are a classic and very simple herbal medicine that you'll find in the cabinets of many herbalists. The following vinegars are examples of what you can make with foraged goods and herbs that you aren't quite sure what to do with. You can make infused vinegar with medicinal or culinary herbs and veggies. It's a great way to preserve summer in a jar for year-round enjoyment.

Garlicky Nettle and Onion-Infused Vinegar

Makes 3 cups

1½ cups tightly packed nettles, coarsely chopped, or 1 cup dried nettle

½ medium sweet onion, coarsely chopped

3 to 5 garlic cloves, coarsely chopped

2 to 3 tablespoons honey, or more depending on taste

3 cups apple cider vinegar

Having a nettle-infused vinegar on hand is always a good idea. It's a lovely way to preserve spring in a jar and keep it on hand year-round. If you have an excess of fresh nettles that are on the brink of wilting to the point of no return, simply stuff 'em in a jar and cover them with some apple cider vinegar. In this recipe you can put the nettles in fresh, without blanching them, as you won't be consuming the actual nettle leaf. I like to use herbal vinegars on salads or when making a simple dressing at home. Anywhere you'd use straight-up vinegar, you can use an herbal-infused one. I always like to use apple cider vinegar for my infusions, but rice or champagne vinegar will also do. Don't hesitate to switch it up with whatever you have on hand or are craving. You will need a cloth or wax paper barrier between the jar mouth and the lid, as vinegars are prone to rusting caps onto the jar. You can get plastic lids for your Mason jars to prevent this as well.

+ + +

Place the nettles, onion, garlic, and honey in a quart-sized jar and cover with vinegar. If using a metal lid, place a square of fabric or wax paper between the jar and the lid. Infuse for 2 to 3 weeks, out of direct sunlight and shaking every few days. Strain the ingredients out if you prefer or keep them in the vinegar. Once done infusing, add more honey if desired. This will keep for up to 1 year in the cupboard.

Mullein Cherry-Huckleberry Syrup

Makes 2 cups

½ cups cherries, rinsed, pits removed

3 cups water

1 cup huckleberries

1 cup tightly packed mullein leaves

1 cup raw honey or cane sugar

Huckleberries usually pop up during that time of summer when smoky skies are gracing us with their presence here in northern Montana. Hands and mouths remain a deep shade of huckleberry purple as the hot, dry days drip though our fingers like pebbles. Each balmy evening lands with a heavy thud as we crash into bed after long hours of work or hiking through the hills. There is a slow, quiet quality of living in Montana, one that my East Coast mind took a long time to adjust to. Breaks are expected, berries are harvested with care and consumed by the handful, and coffee is drunk hot, even on the warmest days.

I first came up with this recipe while working at an outdoor skills camp for kids near Glacier National Park. When the kids would ask me for something to do, I'd often send them out to the brambles surrounding the makeshift kitchen tent to gather huckleberries. It kept them busy until I thought of something else for them to do and provided me with more than enough berries. This was one of the recipes I made when camp was over and I was left with frozen berries to make my own concoctions with.

This syrup is delicious, simple, and perfect for fire season because of the lung-healing nature of mullein (see below). Add an ounce or two to your favorite cocktail or combine with soda water for a healing soda.

✦ ✦ ✦

Place the cherries, water, huckleberries, and mullein in a medium saucepan over medium-high heat. Bring to a boil, then decrease the heat to medium-low, cover the pan, and simmer for 20 to 30 minutes. While the syrup is simmering, add the honey and stir until dissolved. Remove the pan from the heat and strain the liquid into a clean bowl through cheesecloth or a fine mesh strainer. Let cool before transfering to a clean container, then store in the fridge. The syrup will keep for up to 2 months in a securely capped jar or bottle.

All about Mullein

Mullein *(Verbascum thapsus)* is perhaps known best as lung medicine. Identifiable by its fuzzy leaves, yellow flowers, and tall growth (I've seen it get upward of 7 feet), mullein is considered to be an invasive plant, which makes it easy to harvest. Just be wary of pollutants in the immediate area from which you harvest mullein leaves. The yellow mullein flowers that can be harvested in summer can be used to ease earaches when infused into an oil.

Cardamom Cowboy Coffee

Serves 2 to 4

3 cups water

1½ tablespoons crushed cardamom pods

1 cinnamon stick

4 to 6 scoops finely ground coffee

For Connor and me, coffee is a must when camping or spending any period of time outdoors. To us, it doesn't matter how it's made; we just know that we need to have plenty of it. However, this is my favorite method. It's simple and strong and tastes great with baked beans and buttered toast in the morning. It's best made over a fire, but there are no real rules when it comes to cowboy coffee. The amount of coffee you use depends on your preferred strength of flavor. I like mine on the stronger side, served with a little bit of cream.

Place the water, cardamom, and cinnamon in a medium pot over high heat and bring to a boil. Once the water reaches a roaring boil, remove the pot from the heat. Add your desired amount of coffee and stir well. Cover the pot and let the coffee rest for 8 to 10 minutes. Strain and serve warm.

Is your coffee too acidic? Add a small pinch of salt to your brew to mellow out the acidity.

Tulsi and Rosemary-Roasted Tomatoes with Peppered Mushrooms

Serves 2 to 3

Roasted Tomatoes

2 cups cherry tomatoes

1 tablespoon tulsi

1 tablespoon extra-virgin olive oil

2 to 3 garlic cloves, coarsely chopped

1 teaspoon honey

Salt and freshly ground black pepper

2 sprigs rosemary

Peppered Mushrooms

1 heaping tablespoon unsalted butter or ghee

2 cups shiitake mushrooms

1 teaspoon garlic powder

1 teaspoon smoked paprika

Salt and freshly ground black pepper

1 to 2 tablespoons goat cheese, for serving

This is an ode to the first home I ever had on my own. It was a small island cottage with holes in wooden walls that allowed the sea air to leak in all year round. The nights at the cottage by myself were the most memorable. My go-to meal was sautéed tomatoes with a heavy hand of rosemary and half a can of Heinz vegetarian baked beans with lots of sriracha. I didn't have the internet to keep me entertained, so I turned to books, DVDs from the athenaeum, and my trusty old record player. There's something so peaceful and freeing about being on your own for the first time, in a cute little home, surrounded by your belongings and with no one to tell you to do the dishes straight after dinner. Serve with a crusty baguette, goat cheese, and a glass of red wine.

✦ ✦ ✦

To make the tomatoes, preheat the oven to 350°F. Place the tomatoes in a small 8 by 8-inch baking dish and add the tulsi, olive oil, garlic, and honey. Season with salt and pepper to taste. Mix to coat the tomatoes. Once the tomatoes are coated, place the rosemary sprigs on top of the tomatoes and put the pan in the oven. Cook the tomatoes for 10 minutes, stir with a wooden spoon, and cook for another 10 to 15 minutes, until the tomatoes have broken down and are slightly browned.

To make the mushrooms, while the tomatoes are roasting, heat a large pan over medium-high heat. Melt the butter, then add the mushrooms once the pan is hot. Add garlic powder and paprika to the pan, coating the mushrooms. Season with salt and pepper to taste. Make sure that the mushrooms aren't crowding each other and cook for 8 to 10 minutes, until browned and slightly crispy. Once the mushrooms are done, remove the pan from the heat and set it aside till the tomatoes are done.

When the tomatoes are ready, remove them from the oven and add the mushrooms to the baking dish with the tomatoes. Add some goat cheese and eat out of the pan or on a plate as needed. This will keep in the fridge for 3 days.

Fire Season

The moon is ember orange tonight, a holdover from the smoke that's been blanketing the valley these days. The smoke is early this year. My lungs feel itchy and sensitive, as if I've smoked a pack of cigarettes, and my mind itself feels hazed and uncertain. Yesterday, Connor and I drove to the backwoods with hopes of finding some huckleberries. Just moments after I hopped out of the truck, a hopeful paper bag in my hand, I felt dizzy. Before even spotting a huckleberry, we had to turn back to the car.

Fire season is also, in so many ways, a season of anxiety. There's something innately unsettling about the way smoke hangs in the air. It seems to capture the sun and keep a lid on the already hot summer we've been having this year.

I'm beyond frustrated with having to turn back to the truck, but I feel so overcome with fatigue we really don't have a choice. During fire season, you learn to pick and choose your battles with desire, and oftentimes, nature wins out, as it always seems to. There are many reasons to listen to nature and the environment around you. When it's as drastic and sometimes as dire as your immediate forest catching fire, you really need to buckle up, put your human ego aside, and listen to the land around you.

If you happen to live in an area that catches fire every summer, pay close attention to the herbs specific to your lungs and to immediate relief for anxiety. Herbs such as mullein, elecampane, thyme, and slippery elm are fantastic for lungs. You'll want to load up on California poppy, oatstraw, and skullcap to defeat the anxiety that goes along with not feeling able to breathe.

Since staying inside is safest during times like these, I like to blast the AC, put on a mindless television show, and make easy and light dishes like the Shatavari Kale Caesar Salad (page 81) or whip up a batch of Turmeric and Ginger Pickled Eggs (page 134), all while drinking Lemon Balm Mojitos (page 105). You know, to calm the nerves.

Huckleberry-Lavender Sauce

Makes 1½ cups

2 cups huckleberries, frozen or fresh

1 teaspoon dried lavender

½ teaspoon dried thyme

2 tablespoons cane sugar

¼ teaspoon ground cinnamon

¼ teaspoon cocoa powder

¼ teaspoon ground ginger

Huckleberries are a purple and tarter version of wild blueberries. They take hours to harvest in the woods if you're lucky enough to find a spot and sell for upward of $50 a pound at farmers' markets. The whole huckleberry experience reminds me of the lingonberry in Sweden, just more elusive. If you don't happen to live in the northwest region of North America where the huckleberry grows, use blueberries, mulberries, or any other dark berry instead. Serve this sauce with yogurt, oatmeal, or ice cream.

Place all the ingredients in a medium saucepan and cook over medium heat, stirring every few minutes. Once the mixture has begun to boil, turn the heat down to low and let simmer for about 10 minutes longer, or until the berries have started to break down.

You will know that the sauce is done once you can drag a spoon through it and it doesn't flood back to the center right away. Let the sauce cool and store it in a clean pint-sized jar in the fridge. This will keep for up to 2 weeks.

Nettle Tea

Serves 2 to 4

3 cups water

1 cup fresh nettle leaves, or ½ cup dried nettles

The first time I had nettle tea was at the farm I worked on in Sweden. They sold boxes of it in the café and always had some on hand for the workers. I adored the earthy, creamy flavor, and it soon became part of my daily ritual. Nettles are easy to find and identify (see page 39) and even more simple to infuse into hot water for tea. This is a quick and easy version of fresh nettle tea that can be made over a campfire or at home. You put the dried nettles in a muslin tea bag or strain them out once the tea is ready. You can also let this infusion cool and drink it as an iced tea, which is my personal summer favorite.

✦ ✦ ✦

Place the water in a medium pot and bring to a boil over high heat. Once the water reaches a roaring boil, remove the pot from the heat. Add the nettles, cover the pot, and infuse for 20 minutes. Strain the nettle leaves and serve the tea warm or cold.

On Foraging

Here is a list of foraging practices I've picked up over the years. Though this is not a foraging book, herbalism and wildcrafting go hand in hand in many ways, and it's important to educate yourself on ethical and safe practices. I stress this sentiment. Plants are sacred and, in many cases, endangered or vital native species, and they must be treated with respect and consideration.

+ Always harvest less than you think you need. There's nothing worse than letting plants go to waste.

+ Do not overharvest from one plant alone. I like to harvest no more than 10% from a single plant. I suggest floating from plant to plant like a little bee.

+ Educate yourself on both invasive and native plant species in your region. You can find groups, pamphlets, and books to help you on your journey with a quick Google search. United Plant Savers is a fantastic resource for this too.

+ Triple-check your plant BEFORE harvesting and consuming, especially with mushrooms. There are apps, books, and well-practiced foraging friends to help you if you are unsure. My favorite ID app is called Seek.

+ Leave no trace. This is a basic for camping, hiking, and wildcrafting. Always double-check your space before moving on. Leave it just as good as, if not better than, how you found it.

+ Keep paper bags, scissors, and string in your car for spur-of-the-moment harvesting. You never know when you'll come across a patch of luscious clovers or run into a friend who needs some stinging nettle removed from their yard.

+ Find a guidebook that is specific to your region and always carry it with you.

+ Keep in mind that you are a guest in the wild. Be smart and keep a watchful eye for animals or plants such as poison oak/ivy.

+ Be mindful of where you are harvesting. Avoid heavily trafficked roads and trails as well as public parks and playgrounds. Plants are capable of absorbing toxic waste, and pesticides are common in public areas.

+ Watch how you dry herbs, especially mushrooms. I, unfortunately, once got sick and had to call poison control after eating a poorly preserved batch of turkey tail mushrooms. Inspect recently dried herbs and mushrooms for mold and foreign debris. Invest in a dehydrator or screen system to keep drying herbs away from wet areas.

Nettle Flour

2 cups dried nettle   Place the nettles in a clean coffee grinder, small food processor, or blender. Pulse the herb until fine and powdery. Pass through a fine mesh strainer to filter out any remaining herby bits if you prefer an extra fine flour. Store in a clean, airtight jar in the fridge for up to three months.

To Use: When incorporating the nettle flour into a dough or a batter, substitute ¼ cup of the flour in the recipe with ¼ cup nettle flour. If you feel the need to add more nettle flour, be careful of the batter or dough becoming too dry. You may need to add more moisture (water, milk, etc.) as needed. To get a really fine flour, sift the ground nettles through a fine mesh sieve.

Herbal Flour

Herbal flour is a fun and unique way to add some herbal punch and color to doughs and batters for bread, cakes, and pasta. Sure, herbal flour is essentially just an herbal powder, but I like to use it more like a traditional flour for the purpose it serves in food.

When incorporating any herbal flour into a dough or a batter, I substitute ¼ cup of the regular flour in the recipe with ¼ cup herbal flour. If you feel the need to add more herbal flour, be careful of the batter or dough becoming too dry. You may need to add more moisture (water, milk, etc.) as needed. To get a really fine flour, sift the ground herb through a fine mesh sieve. I store my herbal flours in a jar in the fridge for extra longevity. Herbal flours will keep for up to three months in the fridge.

A Small Nettle Cake with Rose Petal Frosting

Serves 3 to 5

Cake

1 cup (2 sticks) unsalted butter, at room temperature

1½ cups cane sugar

1 tablespoon vanilla extract

3 large eggs, at room temperature

2¾ cups all-purpose flour or cake flour

¼ cup Nettle Flour (page 121)

1½ tablespoons matcha

1 tablespoon baking powder

½ teaspoon salt

¼ cup full-fat yogurt

1 cup whole milk, divided

Frosting

1 (16-ounce) can vanilla or cream cheese frosting, at room temperature

½ teaspoon beetroot powder

½ teaspoon Rose Petal Flour (page 121)

1 tablespoon rose water

This is undoubtedly the recipe that I get asked about the most. I've shared my original photo of the cake at least six times on my Instagram, and people really seem to love it. I haven't wanted to share it until I had the right reason to, because, yes, it is just that special. It requires little thought as far as cakes go, but it's the perfect sort to make with your dried herbs, no matter the season. I hate making frosting. It's messy and sticky, and while the homemade stuff may taste better, I still love the frosting that comes in a container and can be consumed at all hours of the day if you really need it. This is a lazy-day cake that still packs a lot of punch. It's made in one large 13 by 18-inch sheet pan, and the shape is cut out as you desire. For example, I used a 4-inch round cake pan to cut out the shapes, but you can make multiple super-mini cakes using the rim of a large glass if you like. One of my favorite cake tricks is brushing milk or syrup (page 76) over the cake before frosting it for ultimate moistness. Sorry if you don't like that word, but get over it because moist is beautiful.

✦ ✦ ✦

To make the cake, preheat the oven to 350°F. Place the butter and sugar in a large bowl and beat using a hand mixer for 4 to 6 minutes, until light and fluffy. Add the vanilla and eggs, incorporating until smooth.

In a separate large bowl, combine the dry ingredients and fluff with a fork or whisk for 30 seconds to 1 minute, mixing until thoroughly combined. Add the dry mix, 1 cup at a time, to the butter mix, along with the yogurt and half the milk. Using a large spoon, or the hand mixer on low, stir until combined. Repeat with the remaining milk.

(continued)

(continued)

Line a 13 by 18-inch sheet pan with parchment paper, greasing the inner edges with butter or nonstick spray. Pour the batter into the pan and spread evenly. Bake for 18 to 20 minutes, until you can insert a toothpick in the center and it comes out clean.

While the cake is baking, make the frosting. Place the frosting in a large bowl, along with the beetroot powder, rose flour, and rose water. Mix until smooth and well combined, adding more beetroot powder for color if desired. Set aside.

Once the cake has completely cooled, cut out the desired shapes with a glass or small cake pan. This is where the size and shape of the cutter you use determines how big your cake(s) will be. Reserve the extra pieces of cake and roll them into small balls for the top. Stack the cake pieces, spreading a spoonful or two of frosting between the layers. Frost the cake and decorate with the cake balls and dried rose petals as desired. It will keep covered in the fridge for up to 5 days.

Wildcrafting and Social Media

Any well-trained herbalist or forager knows not to geotag the spots from which they harvest on social media. We do this in effort to prevent overharvesting and depletion of plants, especially native or endangered species. Not only that, but there are also creatures that depend on these wild plants more than we do, and by making our harvesting location public, there is a chance that we are putting them in harm's way. With the rise of social media herbalists and foragers, there are more and more people out there looking for plants to heal and to eat, which is great but can also encourage poor wildcrafting practices—something no one wants.

So, please, for the sake of the plant world, do not share your harvesting spots on social media. Keep the information within a close circle of people who practice ethical harvesting. Educate yourself and be smart.

Herbed Croutons

Makes 3 cups

3 cups bread, cut or torn into 1-inch pieces

1 teaspoon dried thyme

1 teaspoon dried rosemary

1 teaspoon dried nettle

1 tablespoon minced garlic

½ cup extra-virgin olive oil

Salt and freshly ground black pepper

I'll admit it: I never truly "got" why people like croutons. Maybe it's a holdover from my early 2000s diet culture upbringing, but I used to ask for salads without them. They always just seemed dry and unnecessary to me. However, when I tried my first homemade crouton, I understood the love. They're easy to make and a great way to use up old bread. Plus, they look cute and rustic on top of a salad with some shaved Parmesan. I wouldn't even judge you if you ate them on their own or dipped in some creamy ranch. You do you.

I used a baguette while testing this recipe, but feel free to grab any kind of bread you have lying around your kitchen. English muffins would even work for this! You just want the bread to be thick or an unsliced loaf. I like my croutons a little on the softer side, so I take mine out around the ten-minute mark. Stay close by the oven while these babies are baking so you can test them out as they harden and take them out once they are to your liking.

+ + +

Preheat the oven to 375°F. Place the bread in a medium bowl and coat with the thyme, rosemary, nettle, garlic, and olive oil. Season with salt and pepper to taste. Line a large baking sheet with parchment paper. Spread the coated bread pieces on the baking sheet. Bake for 10 to 12 minutes, until golden brown, turning the croutons halfway through to evenly toast. Remove the baking sheet from the oven and let the croutons cool before serving. Store them in an airtight bag or jar in the cupboard for up to 1 week.

The Perfect Roasted Potatoes

Serves 4 to 6

2 pounds Russet potatoes, washed and cubed, skins on

3 tablespoons dried tulsi

2 tablespoons dried nettles

2 to 3 tablespoons minced garlic

1 tablespoon roasted garlic

¼ cup nutritional yeast

1 tablespoon red pepper flakes

2 to 3 tablespoons oil (olive, coconut, or vegetable)

Salt and freshly ground black pepper

A big go-to in our house is dicing up some potatoes and roasting them with dried herbs. It's one of those put-in-the-oven-set-a-timer-and-forget-about-it sort of recipes that's perfect for busy days or when you want to meal prep. Now, I could be wrong, but I fully believe that nutritional yeast is the key to crispy roasted potatoes. I like to dice potatoes (with the skin on) and spread them out on a large baking sheet. Next, I coat them with oil, herbs, garlic, and lots of nutritional yeast. Pair them with some Herbed Sour Cream (page 61) and you're golden . . . just like your potatoes! If you have any leftovers, fry 'em up with butter and eggs the next morning for an herby potato hash.

✛ ✛ ✛

Preheat the oven to 400°F. Line a large baking sheet with parchment paper. Place the potatoes on the baking sheet and coat them with the herbs, tulsi, nettles, garlic, nutritional yeast, red pepper flakes, and oil. Give the potatoes a good mix with tongs or your hands. Place the baking sheet in the oven and cook the potatoes for 1 hour, flipping them with a spatula halfway through baking. Once the potatoes are crispy and can be punctured with a fork, they are done. Remove the pan from the oven and serve the potatoes warm.

Fall

Fall brings a certain amount of nostalgia to the table. To me, it also marks the start of a new section of my year. Even now, all these years after school has been over, I still get that giddy feeling of starting anew. Beloved sweaters are shaken out of their storage boxes, you get yourself a new book and a new bag to carry it in, and you lace up your favorite pair of leather boots. I love the turnover from summer to fall, and it always seems to bring out a sense of clarity for me. With any luck, the weather has cooled come September, and I can finally get into my kitchen without the dread of sweat and overheating. Spiced baked goods are waiting to be made, and the markets are filled with hearty vegetables that are ready to be preserved and saved for winter.

Perhaps my favorite fall season was when I was nineteen years old, living in a tent on my boss's property, working at a coffee shop I loved, and riding my 1960s green Raleigh all over the island of Nantucket. After a tumultuous summer and an unexpected breakup in Sweden, I came into my own that September. I found a new sense of independence and a feeling of community on the island, and I was more at home than ever. Though I loved living in my tent on the same property as my friends, it was getting cold, and it was time to find a home with actual walls.

I had been approved to live in the NISDA artist cottages on the outskirts of town. The cottages were small, connected by thin walls, and lined up in a large U shape on a small grassy lot across from the harbor. I had been fascinated by the cottages since I was young and was thrilled to be moving into one of my own. My move-in date was October 1, and by that time, I was ready to leave my cold, wet tent. At 11:30 p.m. on September 30, my friends and I packed up my belongings in the tent and threw everything we could into the back of a truck. By 11:50, we piled into the truck and made our way to my new cottage. We waited outside, and once the clock struck midnight, we started moving in. I think we were all excited to have a place, far from our parents, where we could hang out and that we could call our own.

This was the fall when I became an herbalist. When I wasn't working, you could find me wandering around the island with my herb book in my bike basket, scanning the brush and ground for new plants to make medicine with. My tights were constantly ripped from squeezing my way into tight forest corners, and my hair was always dotted with sand or blades of grass. Dried herbs hung on the rafters of my seaside cottage, mostly rosemary, sweet fern, and lavender harvested from gardens around the island. I was finding my way around the kitchen and experimenting with dishes that have since become my go-to comfort meals, such as Tulsi and Rosemary–Roasted Tomatoes with Peppered Mushrooms (page 114).

Fall is a time for finding out what excites us. The weather is cool enough to allow us to think clearly and not feel bogged down by summer bucket lists or suffocating humidity (can you tell I don't like the heat?). It's a time for baking, reading beloved books, and allowing yourself to get cozy and not move for a while or to take a walk and take in the magic of our ever-changing earth. Thinking about all the ways I've evolved during autumn makes me tear up a little bit, if I'm honest with you. Or, perhaps, maybe I'm just a Scorpio.

Chocolate-Covered Figs with Hemp Hearts

Makes 12 to 15 figs

1 (3.2-ounce) bar dark chocolate, coarsely chopped

1 tablespoon coconut oil

¼ teaspoon kosher salt

½ teaspoon ground cinnamon

½ teaspoon ground ginger

16 ounces fresh figs

½ cup hemp hearts

Finishing salt (optional)

Dried rose petals or edible flowers, for garnish

Everyone I know loves a good fig. Even if you aren't fond of the taste, you know you like looking at them. Figs are sweet, plump, and downright sensual. On the outside, figs don't look like anything very special. They're a sort of muddy brown/purple color and could easily be passed over on a serving platter if you didn't know any better. However, once you bite or tear into the little fruit, it's like a whole new world in there. Since figs have such a short season, you can use fresh or dried for this recipe.

Place the chocolate in a double boiler over low heat. Once slightly melted, add the oil, salt, cinnamon, and ginger and fold in gently. Continuously stir until the chocolate is smooth and fully melted. Remove from the heat.

Rinse the figs and cut them in half vertically, starting from the stem. Line a baking sheet with parchment paper. Dip the figs in the melted chocolate, covering them halfway or completely. Repeat until all the figs have been covered in chocolate. Lay the figs on the baking sheet and sprinkle them with the hemp hearts. Sprinkle a small amount of finishing salt on the figs, too, if you'd like. I've also added dried rose petals or edible flowers to some figs for a nice floral pop! Place the figs in the fridge until the chocolate has hardened. The figs will keep for 3 days in the fridge.

Turmeric and Ginger Pickled Eggs

Makes 8 to 10 large eggs

**2 tablespoons grated
fresh turmeric**

**2 tablespoons grated
fresh ginger**

**1 teaspoon ground
turmeric**

**½ tablespoon freshly
ground black pepper**

1½ cups cane sugar

1½ cups water

1½ cups white vinegar

**8 to 10 hard-boiled
large eggs, shelled**

Place all the ingredients except the eggs in a medium pot and bring to a light boil over medium heat. Stir to dissolve the sugar. Remove the pot from the heat and let the mixture cool completely. Place the eggs in a large clean jar or other container. Cover with the vinegar mixture and cover tightly. Place in the fridge for 48 hours before eating.

Pickled Eggs

You may recognize pickled eggs from behind the counter at your favorite local dive bar or beside the register at the corner gas station. And because of this, I feel like pickled eggs have gotten somewhat of a bad rap. The jars are kind of murky and sometimes covered in fingerprints from beer-splattered hands. But please believe me when I say you must give pickled eggs a chance. And I'm here to shed some insight on the best ways to do it. They are more or less the same formula with different flavor profiles.

The longer you allow your eggs to absorb the season, the better they will taste. Always keep the eggs in the vinegar mixture. Pickled eggs will last in an airtight container in the fridge for up to 2 months.

The Coleslaw Egg

Makes 8 to 10 large eggs

1 cup red cabbage,
thinly sliced

1 teaspoon celery seed

½ cup carrots, grated

¼ large red onion,
thinly sliced

1½ cups cane sugar

1½ cups water

1½ cups white vinegar

8 to 10 hard-boiled
large eggs, shelled

Place all the ingredients except the eggs in a medium pot over medium heat and bring to a light boil. Stir to dissolve the sugar. Remove the pot from the heat and let the mixture cool completely. Place the eggs in a large clean jar or other container. Cover them with the vinegar mixture and cover tightly. Place in the fridge for 48 hours before eating.

Beet and Rosehip Eggs

Makes 8 to 10 large eggs

1½ cups white vinegar

1½ cups water

1 (15-ounce) can sliced beets, strained and juice reserved

½ cup whole rosehips, crushed

1½ cups cane sugar

8 to 10 hard-boiled large eggs, shelled

Place the vinegar, water, juice from the can of beets, rosehips, and sugar in a medium pot over medium heat and bring to a light boil. Stir to dissolve the sugar. Remove the pot from the heat and let the mixture cool completely. Place the eggs and the beets in a large clean jar or other container. Cover with the vinegar mixture and cover tightly. Place in the fridge for 48 hours before eating.

The "Perfect" Hard-Boiled Egg

I don't know how to make the perfect hard-boiled egg. I don't believe that anyone truly does. Eggs can have different outcomes depending on their age or size. When hard boiling, try using older eggs (check the expiration date on the carton), as the shells seem to pull away from the whites easier. As for boiling time, I keep it under 10 minutes, usually 9 minutes. Boil water in a large pot and use a spider strainer to carefully drop your eggs in the water once it's reached a roaring boil. Set a timer for 8 to 10 minutes and wait. I've heard that adding a tablespoon of baking soda to your water helps the shelling process, but even after trying this, I can't guarantee it's always true.

After 8 to 10 minutes, remove the eggs from the heat and carefully transfer the eggs to a large bowl filled with cold water and ice cubes. This stops the cooking process and will hopefully leave you with a jammy yolk. Once the eggs have cooled, peel away and you're ready to get pickling!

Crispy Tulsi Chickpeas

Serves 4 to 6

1 (16-ounce) can chickpeas, rinsed and drained

1 tablespoon extra-virgin olive oil

1 teaspoon garlic powder

½ teaspoon red pepper flakes

Salt and freshly ground black pepper

2 heaping tablespoons dried tulsi

These cute little chickpeas are the perfect addition when you need an extra crunch. I started making these a few summers ago, and now I make them whenever I need to jazz up a salad, a pasta dish, or even a soup. While I sadly have to limit my intake of chickpeas (they can cause me some mega endometriosis bloat—gah!), I do occasionally like to treat myself to them. If you cook dried chickpeas with a sheet or two of kombu seaweed, it can possibly help reduce gas and bloat. You can also find canned chickpeas with kombu in them. It's a little extra cost wise but so worth it if you ask me. If you want to avoid chickpeas altogether, try this recipe using another bean that is more to your liking or digestive capabilities. When baking the chickpeas, make sure that none of them are touching, as this will ensure perfectly crisp chickpeas.

Preheat the oven to 350°F.

Line a baking sheet with parchment paper. Place the chickpeas on the baking sheet and coat them with the oil, spices, and tulsi. Spread the chickpeas out, making sure they aren't touching each other.

Bake them in the oven for 8 minutes, then rotate your pan. Bake for an additional 12 minutes, or until crispy. Remove the pan from the oven and let the chickpeas cool. These will keep in an airtight container in the fridge for up to 1 week.

Marionberry and Thyme Chocolate Pie

Serves 8

1½ pounds marionberries

1 cup cane sugar, plus
1 tablespoon, divided

½ cup dark
chocolate chips

1 teaspoons dried
thyme, or 1½ teaspoons
fresh thyme

1 teaspoon cocoa powder

½ teaspoon ground
cinnamon

¼ cup starch (flour,
cornstarch, tapioca, etc.)

1 teaspoon vanilla extract

1 recipe The Only Pie
Crust (page 172)

A Good Egg Wash
(page 173)

This pie was my and Connor's favorite when I was doing my delivery pie service in Missoula. Marionberries paired with the richness of chocolate and the earthiness of thyme make for a wonderful combination of flavors. Be sure to pair this one with a thick yogurt, ice cream, or Floral Whipped Cream (page 176), as it's very rich. If you can't find marionberries at your local market (check the freezer section), use blackberries or a mix of wild berries.

+ + +

Place the berries, 1 cup of the sugar, chocolate chips, thyme, cocoa powder, cinnamon, starch, and vanilla in a large bowl. Combine well, cover with a cloth, and let sit for 20 to 30 minutes. This allows the berries and other ingredients to infuse and get a little syrupy.

While the berry mix is resting, preheat the oven to 400°F. Cut the pie dough in half and roll one half out into a circle about ⅛ inch thick. Lay the dough into a 9-inch pie tin and press into the edges. Poke holes in the dough with a fork, then pour the berry mix over the dough.

Use the remaining half of the dough to decorate the top of the pie as you please. I like to roll the dough out and cut it into half-inch strips to lay over the filling and make braids to surround the pie.

Brush the egg wash over the crust with a pastry brush, then sprinkle the remaining 1 tablespoon sugar over the top. Bake for 1 hour, until the dough is a deep golden brown. Cool before serving.

Gorgonzola-Fig Mac 'n' Cheese

Serves 4 to 6

1 pound small shell pasta

½ cup unsalted butter

¼ cup all-purpose flour

2 cups milk

4 tablespoons fig jam, plus 3 tablespoons, for topping

2 to 3 cloves garlic, minced

1 tablespoon Dijon mustard

1 tablespoon dried thyme, or 1½ tablespoons fresh thyme

1 tablespoon dried rosemary, or 1½ fresh rosemary

1 teaspoon red pepper flakes, or more to taste

5 sage leaves

4 cups shredded cheddar cheese

1 cup Gorgonzola crumbles, divided

1 teaspoon salt

1 teaspoon black pepper

1 cup shredded Parmesan cheese

3 to 4 figs, cut in half lengthwise (optional)

If we've ever met, chances are you know that I'm a sucker for a good cheese board. It doesn't even need to be that fancy for me to fawn all over it. As long as there's a good mix of salty cheese and sweet jams or honey, I'm happy as a lark. (I grew up on Lunchables, and maybe it shows.) My first foray into making mac 'n' cheese from scratch was a few years ago when Connor and I lived above a laundromat in Missoula. Our studio apartment was small, hot, and dark, but we still managed to make some of the best food in that kitchen. The key to good mac 'n' cheese is Dijon mustard, spices, and more cheese than you'd actually expect.

Make this celiac friendly by using your favorite gluten-free pasta and flour mix. My favorite is Bob's Red Mill Gluten Free 1-to-1 Baking Flour.

Preheat the oven to 450°F. Place the pasta in a large pot over high heat and boil according to the instructions on the package. Drain the pasta once cooked and set aside.

Turn the heat to low. In a large heavy-bottomed pot, melt the butter. Once the butter has melted, add the flour, 1 tablespoon at a time, making sure to whisk the mixture continuously. Once the mixture has become a paste-like consistency, add the milk, ½ cup at a time, whisking frequently. When the mixture has become smooth, mix in the fig jam, garlic, Dijon, thyme, rosemary, red pepper flakes, and sage and stir well. Add the cheddar and ½ cup of the Gorgonzola and stir until melted. Add cooked pasta to the mixture and coat evenly. Taste and season with salt and pepper to your liking. Sprinkle the Parmesan and the remaining ½ cup Gorgonzola over the mixture, nestle the fig halves on top, and place the pot in the oven. Cook for 20 minutes, until the top has browned slightly and the mac has set. Broil for an additional 4 to 5 minutes, to get the top extra crispy. Remove from the oven and let cool for 10 minutes before serving. The mac will keep in the fridge for up to 4 days.

Nantucket

Island Call

At the trough, fervid and straw strewn
Sons of fury in their wrinkled frocks and
smoky chords
gunpowder sweet as limes and ginger roots
I rose
one armed with bliss
across each bough of the severed tree the
captain grew
to find
in brambles deep
The beasts –
who roamed my sleepless weeks
These furry beins
well, they cackled and they creeped
across a maze of threads and skins
His dark footed majesty then trickled in
Across my face, his bearded chin did sweep
unseeing seas in goblets blue ran rye and deep
And how could I possibly recall

the Basket, we children had weaved
with cattails, string and furs dandy
brimmed with milk and buds
for I plunged her into Lily's mossy grin
to keep her warm amongst deep pockets in
the sleeves
of Father Fog's Spring cloak
To spare them of foul tastes and unrequited play
my limbs were swept away
Then, did splay, heavy feathered fingers
that slept upon the flesh of my handsome face
My sea bone bellied linings
have recast their woes
of foe and fret
They hunt for beating hides to catch
They leave me peppered raw and stretched
above a pith that dares me not to give
to even Those beneath my chin

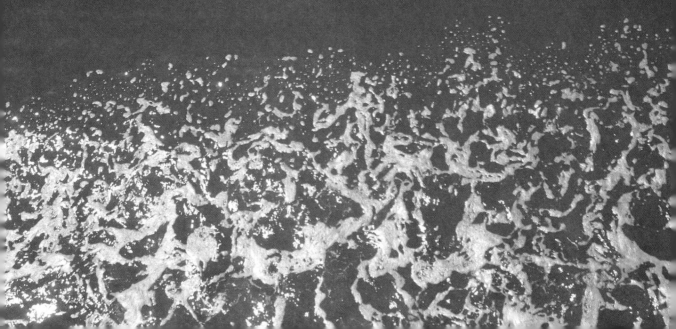

We arrive on the 11:30 slow boat. No matter how many times I've done this, my heart still manages to pitter-patter, and I feel an overwhelming sense of home when the ferry pulls into the harbor. The past few times have been especially emotional. Trips to the island have become far less frequent. Between distance and money, Nantucket has become a place that exists more in memory than reality for me since my dad moved off the island a few years back.

My father, Bob, worked as a chef on Nantucket long before I was around. I moved there in the spring of 1990, fresh as a sprig and soon to be island bound for life in some sense or the other. We moved into the Jared Coffin House, where Dad was recently appointed head chef. The Jared Coffin House (known to some as the J.C.) is most famous for housing Herman Melville during his first trip to Nantucket. Known back then as the Ocean House, the hotel overlooked Captain Pollard's house on Centre Street. Captain George Pollard Jr. was captain of the infamous *Essex* ship. They say Pollard's stories, relayed to Melville, were what inspired Moby Dick; however, Melville himself has said that little more than a few words were exchanged between the two. Regardless of what really happened, there is a sign on Pollard's house that reads "Built by William Brock in 1760. Later owned by Capt. George Pollard, Jun'r of the whaling ship 'Essex.' Herman Melville spoke to Capt. Pollard whose story was the basis for 'Moby Dick,'" thus cementing its place in history.

The Jared Coffin House was my first home. The underbellies of the low tables in the Tap Room, the downstairs restaurant, acted as my forts and hideaways for many a dramatic fit (I was infamous for these as a child and probably still am). The Scottish receptionist, Ms. Bain, let me bug her during the long days when my dad was in the kitchen and entertained me with flamboyant stories, heady gossip, and a love of thrifting during the times I spent at her house outside of the J.C. I loved to roam the hallways of the hotel and somehow managed to do a lot of solo exploration. Prodding half-open doors to peek inside at unmade beds or linen closets and making my best efforts to shimmy down the chestnut railings, I've had a lifelong infatuation with that hotel, simply because it was the first place I came to know as home.

Nantucket is where I came to know and love food in my father's kitchen. The island is where I had my first kiss and where I got high school tipsy off Sprite mixed with green apple vodka in the back of a jeep on a beach. Nantucket to me is as familiar as the inside of my cheek. It's a little painful at times and packs a whole lot of emotion for me, yet I miss it daily. The island has an ability to stir something up inside of you. It'll feed you, nourish you, rip you raw, then take you back again.

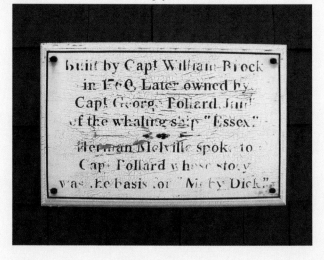

Creamy Adaptogenic Pumpkin Sauce

Makes about 4 cups

1 tablespoon unsalted butter or oil

2 to 3 cloves garlic, minced

2 cups pumpkin puree

1 cup coconut milk (full fat or light, depending on dietary needs)

1 tablespoon adaptogenic powder

1 tablespoon minced fresh rosemary

1 teaspoon minced culinary sage

1 teaspoon allspice powder

2 tablespoons nutritional yeast

½ teaspoon maple syrup

1½ tablespoons sambal oelek

Salt and freshly ground black pepper

There's truly nothing quite like a comforting pumpkin dish in fall. Pumpkin and adaptogens go hand in hand in my opinion, and the powders are easy to incorporate into different sauces. I like to use maca powder for this particular dish, as the nutty flavor of maca pairs well with the sweetness of pumpkin. This recipe is loosely inspired by some amazing curries I've had over the years and have tried to recreate in my own kitchen. It's easy to make and can be added to a wide range of pastas, gnocchi, or roasted veggies. If you double the batch and store it in your fridge for up to 5 days, it makes the perfect addition to meal preps, because we all need a good sauce.

✦ ✦ ✦

Place the butter in a large pan over medium heat. Once the butter has melted, add the garlic and give it a quick stir. Add the pumpkin puree and coconut milk. Once combined, add the remaining ingredients. Simmer the sauce on low for 10 to 15 minutes, stirring occasionally. Once the sauce is thick and tasty, it's ready.

No-Bake Peanut Butter- Reishi Cookies

Makes 12 to 15 cookies

½ cup coconut oil

½ cup peanut butter

½ cup milk, your choice

1 cup raw sugar

¼ cocoa powder

2 tablespoons reishi powder

½ teaspoon kosher salt, if using saltless peanut butter

1 teaspoon vanilla extract

3¼ cups rolled oats

Edible flowers (cornflower, rose petals, calendula, lavender), for garnish

This is my herbalist's take on the no-bake cookies I grew up eating. Every so often, my mom would make a big batch of these oat cookies and line the kitchen counter with them while they cooled. They are my ultimate comfort cookie. Keep in mind that because these cookies are made with coconut oil, they have a tendency to melt, so store them in a cool spot. These also freeze really well!

Place the coconut oil, peanut butter, milk, sugar, cocoa powder, reishi powder, and salt (if using) in a large saucepan over medium heat. Stir constantly until the mixture comes to a roaring boil. Decrease the heat and let simmer for about 4 minutes, stirring occasionally, making sure to scrape the sides and bottom.

Once the mixture has come together into a thick, shiny sauce, remove the saucepan from the heat and add the vanilla. Add the oats and mix fully to combine.

Line a baking sheet with parchment paper. Drop large spoonfuls (about 2 tablespoons each) of the mixture onto the sheet. These cookies do not have to be perfect by any means, but try to get them into an oval or rounded shape. Sprinkle edible flowers on the cookies while they are still wet. Place the baking sheet in the fridge and let the cookies set for at least 45 minutes. These will keep for up to 5 days in the fridge.

Dad's Quahog Chowder

Serves 4 to 6

½ cup unsalted butter

1 cup diced yellow onion

1 cup diced fennel root

2 teaspoons finely chopped garlic

¼ cup all-purpose flour

1 cup clam juice

2 cups Plant Magic Broth (page 175) or non-herbal broth

1 cup peeled and diced Russet potatoes

1½ cups chopped quahog meat

1½ teaspoons chopped fresh thyme

2 bay leaves

2 cups light cream or half-and-half

Salt and freshly ground black pepper

Fennel fronds, for garnish

Crackers of choice, for serving

Growing up on the coast, you tend to eat a lot of chowder. Clam chowder is classic, seafood chowder is always a good choice, but quahog chowder is *chef's kiss.* Quahogs are clams that are local to the cape and islands. Their smaller, more common cousin is called the littleneck, though they are essentially the same thing from what I understand. Quahogs are a Nantucket specialty and are easy to find on menus all across the island. You can also use canned chopped clams if quahogs or littlenecks are unavailable. Chef Bob (my dad) suggests that you stir in a half dash each of Tabasco and Worcestershire sauce and serve with oyster crackers or saltines.

+ + +

Place the butter in a large heavy-bottomed pot over medium heat. Once melted, add the onion and fennel. Stir with a whisk for about 6 minutes, until the onions are translucent. Add the garlic and stir until fragrant. Stir in the flour with a whisk, making a roux. Cook for 3 minutes, stirring occasionally.

Add the clam juice, broth, potatoes, quahog, thyme, and bay leaves. Turn the heat down to low and simmer for about 8 minutes, until the potatoes become just tender. Stirring occasionally, make sure to scrape the bottom of the pot, then whisk in the cream and simmer for 2 minutes. Season to taste with salt and pepper. Garnish with some fennel fronds and serve warm with crackers.

Rosehip Hot Honey

Makes 1½ cups

1½ cups honey

1 to 2 tablespoons
red pepper flakes

¼ cup crushed
rosehips, dried

Okay, so maybe this should be called "rosehip hot-ish honey" because to me, it's not all that spicy. I'm the type to put hot sauce on everything I eat. I carry a bottle around in my car in case there is some sort of bland food emergency that must be remedied. However, with this one, I like to keep it a little mild so that the rosehips have some space to shine. If you want to spice it up, add a dried hot pepper or two. I like to leave the herbs in the honey, but you can strain them out while the honey is still warm by using a fine mesh strainer. It will take some time to strain the honey, so don't rush the process! Pair the honey with a cheese board or drizzle it on top of pizza, which is my favorite move.

+ + +

Place the honey, red pepper flakes, and rosehips in a small saucepan over low heat and bring to a gentle simmer. Remove the pan from the heat, cover, and let sit for 1 hour. Strain the honey through a fine mesh strainer into a clean vessel. Cover and store at room temperature for up to 1 month.

Cinnamon-Sugar Cheesecake with Gingersnap Crust

Serves 6 to 8

2 cups crushed
gingersnaps

1 tablespoon grated
fresh ginger

1 cup unsalted
butter, melted

4 (8-ounce) packages
cream cheese, at room
temperature

6 large eggs

1½ cups cane sugar

½ cup sour cream

1 tablespoon ground
cinnamon

¼ tablespoon ground
nutmeg

1 tablespoon all-
purpose flour

1 teaspoon salt

1 teaspoon vanilla extract

I first learned how to make cheesecake while working at Café Rosenhill in Sweden. After just a few days of weeding in the sunny field, my skin turned a vicious, flakey red. Emilia, the farm owner, looked me up and down and said flatly, "We will move you to the kitchen." Sadly, my days as a farmer were numbered, but my move to the kitchen was what introduced me to my love of cooking and baking. From then on, I spent morning to evening in the kitchen of the café, or gathering wild blueberries and lingonberries in the forest just off the property. Emilia let me whip up whatever creations came to mind and forgave me when I put salt instead of sugar in the kladdkaka (chocolate cake). Maybe Emilia saw something of herself in me, which caused her to be so accepting, or maybe it was the fact that her son and I had fallen head over heels in love with each other. I was swiftly moved from my bus into their big yellow house. Either way, I credit Emilia for my love and passion for using unique and herbal ingredients.

Once upon a time, Emilia had her own cooking show. She could incite a raging round of song and deep-bellied laughter. She was a force to be reckoned with. Before her death, her treatments weren't working as everyone had hoped, and a friend told me that Emilia claimed it was because she had dragon's fire and blood in her veins. I miss her daily, but I take solace and find bits of her memory in my own kitchen and garden.

Cinnamon and ginger are two of those classic spices that are fiery yet comforting. Combined with the sweetness of cheesecake, it sort of reminds me of Emilia and her comforting nature. I also just don't like traditional graham cracker crust. This cake is a blend of everything hearty and comforting. Enjoy it with a fiery friend. Make this a day ahead of time to allow the cake to set properly in the fridge.

+ + +

Preheat the oven to 400°F. Place the gingersnaps, ginger, and butter in a medium bowl. Mix until the ingredients stick together. Line a 10-inch springform pan with a layer of parchment paper, making sure to crease the paper in the edges of the pan as much as possible. Transfer the gingersnap mixture to the pan and, using your hands, spread it out as evenly as possible.

In a large bowl, combine the cream cheese, eggs, sugar, sour cream, cinnamon, nutmeg, flour, salt, and vanilla using a handheld mixer for about 5 minutes, or until smooth. Once combined, transfer the mixture to the pan, distributing it evenly over the crust. Place the pan in the oven for 45 to 50 minutes, until the top of the cheesecake has browned. Remove the pan from the oven and let the cheesecake cool to room temperature, then store overnight in the fridge. Serve cold or at room temperature.

The cheesecake will keep for up to 1 week in the fridge.

Golden Milk Chocolate Bark

Serves 6 to 8

2 cups white chocolate chips

1½ tablespoons turmeric

1 teaspoon ground ginger

1 teaspoon ground cinnamon

¼ teaspoon freshly ground black pepper

Pinch of salt

Rose petals, calendula, chopped nuts, sunflower seeds, for garnish

This recipe is beyond simple while conveying the illusion of taking great skill. Give it as a gift or wow your friends after dinner by serving this on a plate with coffee or tea. Be warned: this will melt if left somewhere warm for too long! It's best kept in the fridge or freezer. Take extra measures to make sure that no water or excess liquid gets into the chocolate during the cooking process, as it will cause the chocolate to clump. You can read more about the traditional use of Golden Milk on page 37. When garnishing chocolate bark, I like to use chopped nuts, sunflower seeds, or dried edible flowers. How much you use is really up to you, but I keep the nuts and seeds to about ¼ cup and 2 tablespoons or so of each dried flower.

+ + +

Place a double boiler over low heat. Melt the white chocolate chips in the bowl while stirring continuously with a rubber spatula or wooden spoon. Once the chocolate has melted, stir in the remaining dry ingredients, reserving the garnishes. Stir until well combined, then remove the pot from the heat.

Line a baking sheet with parchment paper. Evenly spread the chocolate over the baking sheet, then garnish with your desired toppings. Place the sheet in the fridge for about 1 hour, or until the chocolate has completely hardened.

Once solid, break the chocolate into pieces with the handle of the wooden spoon or spatula. Keep the bark in resealable bags or containers and store in the fridge or freezer. It will keep in the fridge for 2 weeks and in the freezer for 3 months.

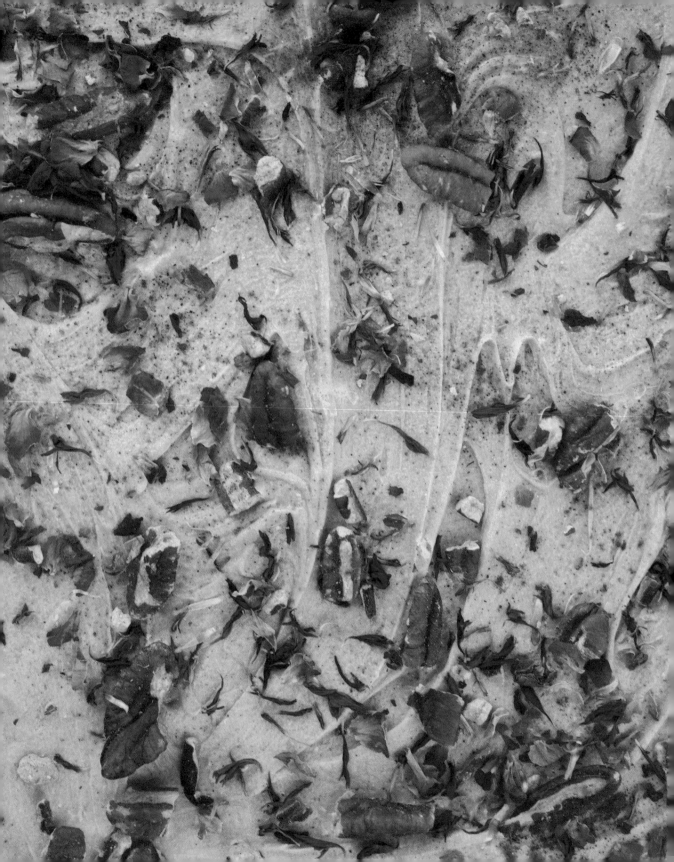

Stewed Pears with Rose Petal Sauce

Serves 4

4 cups water

3 cinnamon sticks

1 teaspoon ground ginger

1 teaspoon ground cardamom

1 cup firmly packed dark brown sugar

1 teaspoon vanilla extract

1 cup cane sugar

4 pears (any kind will do), peeled

¼ cup dried rose petals

½ cup heavy cream

This dish was inspired by one of the most magical movies I've ever seen, Like Water for Chocolate. *There is a scene in both the movie and the book where Tita, lovesick and full of passion, makes a meal of quail in rose petal sauce. It is so full of emotion that when her sister, Gertrudis, eats it, she becomes overheated and full of passion herself. She runs to the shower to cool off but is so filled with heat that the wooden shower stall and her clothes burn up. Gertrudis is swept up by a man on a horse and carried away to a life of passion. You can find the actual recipe for the quail in the book that the movie was based on, but this sweet pear version is my own dessert version of it. These pears taste great warm with some ice cream or cold on their own but are best shared with a lover.*

✛ ✛ ✛

Place the water and cinnamon sticks in a Dutch oven or large lidded pot over medium heat. Cover and bring to a boil for 10 minutes.

Next, add the ginger, cardamom, brown sugar, vanilla, and sugar. Cover and boil for 10 to 15 minutes, until the liquid has thickened slightly and has reduced by ½ inch or so.

Add the pears and rose petals. Decrease the heat to low, cover the pot, and cook the pears for 20 minutes, rotating every 5 minutes. The pears are done when you can easily slide a knife or fork into the fruit.

Once the pears are ready, slowly incorporate the cream, about 1 tablespoon at a time, stirring constantly. Remove the pot from the heat and serve the pears warm or cold.

Adaptogenic Pumpkin Pop Tarts

Makes 12 to 15 tarts, depending on size

Filling

1 (15-ounce) can pumpkin puree

1 tablespoon maca powder or reishi mushroom powder

1 teaspoon ground cinnamon

¼ cup brown sugar

½ teaspoon ground nutmeg

¼ teaspoon freshly ground black pepper

1 tablespoon minced fresh ginger

½ teaspoon ground cloves

1 recipe the Only Pie Crust (page 172)

Glaze

1 cup confectioners' sugar

1 heaping tablespoon ground cinnamon

3 to 5 tablespoons milk, your choice

Sprinkles (optional)

I made these pop tarts for the release party of my first book, in the fall of 2018. They were a hit, and my cousin Stephanie has been eager to get her hands on the recipe. Both fun and perfectly autumnal, these little tarts are ideal for a quick-ish baking project. With the addition of a powdered adaptogenic herb, they can even be considered. . . healthy-ish. Use the pie crust recipe on page 172 for this or feel free to buy one too. There's no shame in saving some time, and it's more important that you make something fun to eat with prebought dough than having anxiety over making your own. Cut them into any shape or size you'd like; just make sure to seal the edges with a fork to prevent leaking. I always use canned pumpkin puree for this recipe, but if you prefer to use canned pumpkin pie mix, that's up to you! Either way, you'll be adding similar ingredients, so keep it as pumpkin pure as possible, if you can. Oh! I prefer to make my own powdered sugar, as I think it tastes better. To do this, blend 2 cups of cane sugar to get roughly 1½ cups of confectioners' sugar. You can blend the sugar in a food processor or, my favorite, the Magic Bullet. But you can, of course, just buy powdered sugar at the store too.

+ + +

Preheat the oven to 350°F. Place the pumpkin, maca, cinnamon, brown sugar, nutmeg, pepper, ginger, and cloves in a large bowl and combine. Roll the dough out to ¼ inch thick. Cut as many 2 to 3-inch rectangles as you have room for, using a butter knife or a cookie cutter if you have one. Place 1 teaspoon of the filling onto the bottom half of a rectangle. Using another dough rectangle, sandwich the filling and press a fork around the edges to keep the filling in. Make sure to poke 2 to 3 holes on the top of the tart using the fork or a toothpick. Repeat with the remaining dough and filling.

Line a baking sheet with parchment paper. Place the tarts on the baking sheet and bake them for 25 minutes, or until the dough has become golden brown. Remove the baking sheet from the oven and let the tarts cool completely before adding the glaze.

While the tarts are baking, make the glaze. Add the confectioners' sugar and cinnamon to a small bowl and fluff with a fork or small whisk. Once combined, add the milk, 1 tablespoon at a time, whisking continuously. Once the glaze has become thick and smooth, dip the cooled tarts into the mixture or drizzle it over with a spoon. Transfer the tarts to a cooling rack and let the glaze harden. If using sprinkles, add them immediately after the glaze is applied.

Serve the pop tarts at room temperature. Keep them in an airtight container in the fridge for up to 1 week or freeze them for up to 1 month.

Nettle Pasta

Serves 4 to 6

¼ cup Nettle Flour
(page 121)

1 teaspoon kosher salt

2¾ cups all-purpose flour

4 large eggs, at room
temperature

The first time I made nettle pasta, my heart grew three sizes larger due to the pride I felt over such a fine dish. The long noodles were a deep shade of green that can only be described as ethereal, and they tasted like a warm, witchy hug. The thing that I've learned about pasta is that you really have to trust your intuition while making it. The kneading process is a little long winded, giving you the time to get to know the feel of the dough. Using your hands to work with food is one of my favorite aspects of cooking. There is so much love and passion that goes into the food that nourishes us, especially when it comes to handmade pasta. I've made my fair share of faulty pasta at home, so remember to not be too hard on yourself. Head to YouTube and familiarize yourself with kneading techniques (Pasta Grannies is my favorite channel for this!).

Serve nettle pasta with butter, garlic, and Tulsi and Rosemary–Roasted Tomatoes with Peppered Mushrooms (page 114) or make a carbonara drowned in shaved Parmesan. Substitute nettles with other herbs such as tulsi or even rose petals (see page 121).

+ + Hot Tips + +

Fresh pasta needs
to cook for only
2 to 3 minutes!
Boil it in salted water
as you normally
would. Frozen pasta
will need a few extra
minutes to cook.
For a deeper colored
pasta, substitute an
additional ¼ cup of
herbal flour for the all-
purpose flour.

+ + +

Place all the ingredients in a large bowl and combine. Add a little olive oil to your hands and combine the mixture with your hands until the dough is shaggy in texture.

Next, dump the dough onto the countertop and knead it for about 10 minutes, until it is smooth and elastic-like. Cover the dough with plastic wrap and let it rest for 30 minutes.

After 30 minutes, cut the dough into halves or quarters and roll them out to ¼ inch thick. Cut as desired or process through a pasta maker. You can also freeze the pasta on a baking sheet, then transfer it to a storage container once the pasta is completely frozen. The pasta will keep in the freezer for up to 2 months.

Sage Margarita

Makes 1 drink

Coarse salt

Ice cubes

1½ ounces tequila,
your choice

1 ounce Sage Simple
Syrup (page 84)

1 ounce orange liqueur

1 ounce freshly
squeezed lime juice

Coarse salt and lime
wedges, for garnish

This is a drink that I like to make year round, but there's something really nice and autumnal about making it throughout the fall. Sage margs are a great alternative to all those pumpkin- and apple-flavored drinks you so often see this time of year and are easy to whip up in a pitcher for all your friends. Simply multiply the recipe by however many people you want to serve. I like to rim my glass with a coarse, smokey salt for extra drama. The best way to rim a glass with salt is to evenly distribute 2 tablespoons salt on a small plate, then wet the rim of a glass with a lime and place it upside down in the salt. Make sure it's coated to your liking before pouring the drink.

+ + +

Salt the rim of your glass and fill with ice cubes. Add the tequila, sage syrup, orange liqueur, and lime juice, then stir well. Garnish with a lime wedge and serve right away.

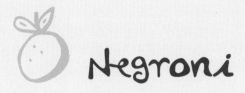

Negroni

Makes 1 drink

1 ounce Campari

1 ounce sweet vermouth

1 ounce gin

Ice

Orange peel, for garnish

Negronis are, hands down, my favorite cocktail, and they definitely feel like one of the herbier cocktails. On my wedding night, I notoriously spilled one down the front of my white linen dress halfway through dinner. Luckily, my maid of honor, Maria, always quick on her feet, immediately ordered a seltzer to remove the spill, and the dress was saved. Negronis are S-T-R-O-N-G and best enjoyed before a meal. Serve these in a rocks glass, never a martini glass. Martini glasses are a recipe for disaster, in my opinion.

+ + +

Pour the Campari, vermouth, and gin into a tumbler filled with ice. Give it a quick stir, then strain the liquid into a rocks glass. Garnish with a sliver of fresh orange peel.

Winter

Winter is often fierce and lonesome, yet when banded wholly and lovingly, majestic verse is exchanged in ways that make the cold feel warm to our ever small hands that are always within reach of one another.

Cabin fever is setting in. It's early March, and I'm sick of the snow and relentless cold winds. After a few failed attempts to make the most of winter that include a poorly thought out car camping trip and a drive that got us (and the tow truck) stuck in the snow for six hours, I am done with winter. True, we got lucky this year with the late start to the snowfall, but five weeks of hard winter in Montana is exhausting to me, and I need to get out of the house. March is affectionately called "hate month" back home on Nantucket, as it's the time when people are sick of the cold and sick of the same old people. I'm feeling this heavily right now, just minus the seeing people part.

This is our first winter at the cabin, and while it's been cozy, it is also very trying for my mental health, especially with the unexpected loss of our sweet cat, Bathory. In Missoula, we were able to leave our tiny studio apartment on foot and walk to the movies, a brewery, or a restaurant whenever we felt like it. But here, an hour and a half from the city, our options are limited. It takes time to get anywhere, and with my anxiety about snow driving, I sometimes feel stuck out here. As an extrovert who grew up in cities and town centers, this rural spot feels a little bit foreign to me. So after a small argument and a little bit of thought, we head to one of the bars in town.

After some small talk with the bartender about cabin fever and the weather, we run into Connor's friend who lives above the bar. He's a wildland firefighter, and he's got the energy to match. He buys us both a drink, challenges Connor to a game of pool, and convinces us both to burn a $20 bill in the wood-burning stove that sits next to the casino game machines in the bar. He grumbles about how money is rooted in evil and bullshit, and after some coaxing, he gets me to toss the bill he handed me into the fire. This is my first time fully experiencing the local bar scene in our new town, and it's really living up to the Wild West image of Montana I know so many people have. After last call, we find ourselves in the apartments upstairs, drinking whiskey and attempting to one-up each other with stories about our lives. Everything is hazy, and the tales get more outlandish as the night moves into morning.

The next day, I wake up with a dull ache all over my body. The blue light of winter has long since crept its way into our loft. Normally, I feel guilty about drinking like that (I'd like to thank my Irish Catholic ancestors for the guilt), but considering how long I've been inside and how rough this winter has been, I laugh it off and make myself a cup of coffee and heat the pan to make some toast. The mountains are glowing and look sharp as glass today, and I think to myself, "Maybe winter isn't as hard as it was yesterday. Maybe I can get through this after all."

Blueberry-Lavender Pie

Serves 8

1½ pounds blueberries

1 cup cane sugar, plus 1 tablespoon for topping, divided

1 tablespoon dried lavender flowers

3 tablespoons cornstarch, tapioca starch, or flour

½ teaspoon ground cinnamon

1 tablespoon cocoa powder

1 teaspoon ground ginger

Pinch of ground nutmeg

1 recipe the Only Pie Crust (page 172)

A Good Egg Wash (page 173)

When it grows cold, I take to baking pies, a ritual that has brought me so much bliss during the snowy season. This pie has been a household favorite and was the most ordered item when I ran my pie delivery service in Missoula. It was first created when Connor brought home a surplus of frozen blueberries from the natural food store he once worked at.

Deeply satisfying and rich, with the bitter brightness of Montana-grown lavender, this pie is bound to please and lead to silence as the flavors roll over your tongue. The lavender complements the berries without overpowering it and may even cause your mind to drift off to warmer days. Though, to me, lavender has always seemed most appropriate for the cool moments of winter. Lavender is warming, aids digestion, and can act like an old friend you've known since childhood. Serve with Floral Whipped Cream (page 176) or a big dollop of full-fat yogurt.

✦ ✦ ✦

Place the blueberries, 1 cup of the sugar, lavender, cornstarch, cinnamon, cocoa powder, ginger, and nutmeg in a large bowl and mix well. Cover and allow the mix to rest for 30 minutes to let the flavors infuse.

While the mix is resting, preheat the oven to 400°F. Cut the pie dough in half and roll one half out into a circle about ⅛ inch thick. Lay the dough into a 9-inch pie tin and fit it around the edges. Poke holes in the dough with a fork, then pour the berry mix over the crust.

Use the remaining half of the dough to decorate the top of the pie as you please. I like to roll the dough out and cut it into half-inch strips to lay over the filling and make braids to surround the pie.

Brush the egg wash over the crust with a pastry brush, then sprinkle the remaining 1 tablespoon sugar over the top. Bake for 1 hour, until the dough is a deep golden brown. Cool before serving.

The Only Pie Crust

Makes two 9-inch pie crusts

3 cups all-purpose flour

½ teaspoon salt

2 tablespoons cane sugar

2 sticks unsalted butter, very cold, cut into ½-inch cubes

1 cup water, ice cold, divided

This is my tried-and-true recipe for pie crust. Before I started making pies for my pie delivery service—and, hopefully, one day, café, Lion & Ram— I was admittedly terrified of pie crust. For years, I'd heard tales of the "best ways to make crust" and how you need to use certain secret ingredients to make the greatest one. But I'm here to tell you to just get over your fears and make a damn pie crust! I'm not exaggerating when I say that making that first pie changed my life. It opened up a world that showed me people are so invested in a good pie, whether you buy it to eat or click "like" on a photo. After a few months, I suddenly became the go-to pie person and was making them left and right. If you want to add some herbs to the crust à la the Garlicky Tomato Galette with Herbed Crust and Chèvre recipe on page 94, add a heaping tablespoon of whatever dried herb you'd like to the flour mix before incorporating the butter. I like to use herbs like nettles, tulsi, or dried rose petals.

+ + +

Place the flour, salt, and sugar in a large bowl and whisk to incorporate. Add the butter, then combine the mixture with your hands until the dough is coarse and crumbly. Add 4 tablespoons of the water and continue to mix with your hands, adding more water if the dough is dry. Once the dough is sticky, form it into a ball, then roll it out to form a small disk. Wrap the dough with plastic wrap and keep it in the fridge for 1 hour or overnight before using.

A Good Egg Wash

Makes enough for 2 to 4 pies

1 large egg, beaten

½ teaspoon water

While an egg wash isn't necessarily essential, it IS important if you want to make your baked goods shine . . . like, literally shine. By brushing a bit of egg wash over the top of your dough before baking, you add a little extra crunch and that lovely pastry sheen that makes your baked goods eye-catching and pretty.

+ + +

Place the egg in a small cup or bowl and add the water. Using a mini whisk or a fork, combine the egg and the water. Use immediately to brush onto unbaked dough and pastries. It will keep in the fridge for 24 hours.

Plant Magic Broth

Serves 6 to 8

8 to 10 slices astragalus

5 slices reishi mushroom

1 to 2 full heads garlic, halved crosswise (skin on)

2 tablespoons chopped fresh ginger

2 tablespoons chopped fresh turmeric

1 sheet kombu

1 teaspoon black peppercorns

1 large yellow or red onion, cut into quarters (skin on)

1 large carrot, cut or thinly sliced

1 cup fresh mushrooms, your choice

2 tablespoons dried rose petals

½ cup dried nettles, or 1 cup fresh nettles

This broth is an ode of love to that simple wild stew we made so long ago. It's a simple way to get your herbs in or use up any produce that is on the brink of spoiling. While this broth is plant based, feel free to add stock bones or leftovers from a roasted chicken. As always, remember to improvise and use what you have or have access to. This is a very forgiving recipe. Astragalus root (Astragalus membranaceus) is a warming adaptogenic herb that is specific for strengthening immunity and encouraging a healthy metabolism and digestive system. I like to add astragalus for an immune-boosting punch to anything from broth to teas to rice. Keep in mind that astragalus is not recommended during pregnancy or while taking immune-suppressing medications. If the use of astragalus is not recommended for you, simply skip it!

Place all the ingredients in a heavy-bottomed pot and cover with water, up to 2 to 3 inches below the rim. Cook over low heat for 3 to 4 hours. Add salt and other spices to taste. Once you are satisfied with the taste, strain the broth. Store it in airtight jars in the fridge for up to 1 week or freeze in ice cube trays or freezer-safe bags for longer storage. You can compost the used veggies and herbs or freeze them to make a second batch (just make sure to add a little more garlic and onions and refresh the herbs).

Floral Whipped Cream

Makes 2 cups

Makes 2 cups

1 cup heavy whipping cream

1 teaspoon orange blossom water

2 tablespoons cane sugar

1 tablespoon rose petals

1 tablespoon calendula

1 teaspoon cornflower

Ugh, give me a spoon and I'll eat this stuff like pudding. There's nothing better than homemade whipped cream. As a Waldorf kid in Maine, we were taught to appreciate the stuff at a young age. Every time a classmate had a birthday, we were served the same gingery birthday cake with a huge glob of sugar-free whipped cream on the side. I can still recall the comforting flavor and the smoke as one of my classmates blew out the rainbow beeswax birthday candles. (We'd try to catch the smoke in our hands while yelling, "Smoke fairies!" like the whimsical Waldorf kids we were trained to be.) Nothing was better than a birthday at school back then. This is my updated take on whipped cream. It's got just as much whimsy and flowers to boot. Serve this on top of the Blueberry-Lavender Pie (page 170) or atop the Lavender-Matcha Iced Latte (page 64). You can use dried or fresh flowers for this recipe, but for the sake of ease, I'm using dried here. You can find orange blossom water in most markets and specialty stores these days and, of course, online. If rose water is all you have on hand, use that! It's just as delicious.

+ + +

Place the cream, orange blossom water, and sugar in a large bowl. Using a hand mixer, mix for 4 to 5 minutes, until stiff peaks are formed. Once the whipped cream is ready, gently fold in the rose petals, calendula, and cornflower. Store in a jar or in an airtight container with plastic wrap pressed down onto the surface of the cream to prevent separation and a film from forming on the top. This will keep in the fridge for up to 3 days.

Make a Japanese fruit sandwich by placing a good-sized dollop of whipped cream on two slices of white bread, adding cut fruit, and removing the crusts. So cute and fun!

Catching Our Food

Nantucket, MA

It was a spur-of-the-moment decision, this grand feast of ours. We got it into our heads to go forth and put our fledgling foraging skills to the test. We wanted to try our hand at gathering all the ingredients for the finest meal we've ever made. My kitchen was closest, so that was our designated cooking spot. I hurried home to prepare the dishes and wait for lanky island boys to bring me their gathered goods. The boys came through with their bounty and dropped everything on the counter in front of me.

At the time, I wasn't all that comfortable in the kitchen just yet, but we poked and prodded our way through the goods: young cattails, periwinkles, various grasses, and mollusks—all talismans from our childhoods on Nantucket yet new to our plates. After some debate, we decided that our best bet was a stew. Throwing things into a pot and adding spices is perhaps the most foolproof way to make the best out of whatever ingredients you have on hand. So into the stockpot our dirt and sea treasures went. It was consumed with toasted bread, joy, and complete admiration of the island we lived on.

Roasted Grapes with Floral Goat Cheese

Serves 2 to 4

Grapes

2 cups seedless grapes, washed and dried, stems removed

¼ red onion, cut into ½-inch slices

1 teaspoon balsamic vinegar

Pinch of red pepper flakes

1 sprig fresh rosemary

2 tablespoons extra-virgin olive oil

Salt and freshly ground black pepper

Floral Goat Cheese

5 ounces soft chèvre, at room temperature

1 teaspoon dried or fresh calendula petals

½ teaspoon dried rose petals

½ teaspoon cornflower

Honey

Fresh violets, for garnish

One of my favorite grape moments in cinematic history is from Under the Tuscan Sun, *when Diane Lane's character beautifully describes a Tuscan market. "I eat a hot grape from the market, and the violet sweetness breaks open in my mouth. It even smells purple," she pens in a failed postcard-writing effort for a fellow tourist. I think of this often and how perfectly that nails the "dream grape experience." This recipe is a little ode to the grape, which I believe gets overlooked too often in savory cooking. I prefer purple grapes when making this dish, but white grapes are perfectly fine if that's all you have on hand. Make sure they are seedless unless you don't mind pulling seeds out of your teeth every other bite. This is a rich little dish, so you'll want to be sure to share with friends. Serve atop crusty bread or crackers, chicken, or a roasted portobello mushroom. PS. This also makes an excellent sandwich schmear.*

✛ ✛ ✛

Preheat the oven to 450°F. Place the grapes, onions, vinegar, red pepper flakes, and rosemary in a medium oven-safe dish. Cover with the oil and your desired amount of salt and pepper, then mix to coat the grapes. Roast them in the oven for 20 minutes.

To make the floral goat cheese, while the grapes are roasting, put the chèvre, calendula, rose, and cornflower in a small bowl. Stir until the cheese and flowers are combined. Add the honey to your desired sweetness and continue mixing.

After 20 minutes, remove the grapes from the oven and give them a good stir. Spoon large dollops of the goat cheese on top of the grapes and return the dish to the oven. Roast for another 10 to 15 minutes, until the chèvre has browned slightly. Serve warm with a few fresh violets on top.

Roasted Root Salad

Serves 4 to 6

½ cup unsalted butter or coconut oil

3 cloves garlic, crushed

1 teaspoon dried thyme

½ teaspoon smoked paprika

Salt and freshly ground black pepper

1 tablespoon maple syrup

2 large carrots

2 large parsnips

2 large burdock roots

Flakey finishing salt

Fennel fronds, for garnish

I'm a real sucker for "rustic" dishes. I appreciate the simplicity they evoke and the traditional use of ingredients. Roasted roots are, to me, the epitome of all things hearty and rustic. Plus, they're easy as pie to make.

We aren't going to peel these roots, because it's not something I do in my own kitchen. But if you must, then go for it. It's all in your hands, little pumpkin. I'm just here for suggestions. Just make sure to give them all a proper scrub, especially the burdock. I've tested this recipe using both butter and coconut oil, so you can pick whatever works best for you.

+ + +

Preheat the oven to 450°F. Place the butter, garlic, thyme, paprika, salt, pepper, and maple syrup in a large skillet over medium-low heat. Stir until the butter has melted and becomes ever so slightly browned or until the oil is warmed.

Remove the sauce from the heat and begin to prep the roots by rinsing and removing the green tops. Line a baking sheet with parchment paper. Carefully slice the roots lengthwise down the middle and place them on the baking sheet.

Pour the sauce over the roots, making sure to fully coat them. Place the baking sheet in the oven for 20 minutes, until you can easily poke a fork through the roots. Once out of the oven, finish with some flakey salt and a few fennel fronds on top. Serve the vegetables warm or cold.

Burdock and Parsnip Puree

Serves 4 to 6

2 tablespoons unsalted butter

½ pound parsnips, peeled and sliced thin

½ pound fresh burdock roots, peeled and sliced thin

½ cup whole milk

½ cup heavy cream

1 tablespoon fresh thyme

3 to 5 cloves garlic, peeled, whole

Salt and freshly ground black pepper

Fresh burdock root, when roasted and seasoned well, is one of my favorite ways to consume a good digestive herb. While earthy and slightly bitter, burdock root brings a really nice, unique flavor to the table while being great for you. This puree is comforting and perfect for colder months, when our digestive tracts are moving slowly and leafy greens are less present. Serve this puree with a hearty piece of salmon or on toast with some mushrooms and microgreens. You'll end up just as obsessed as I am.

Place the butter in a large pot over medium heat. Once the butter has melted, add the parsnips and burdock slices, then cover them with the milk and cream. Add the thyme, garlic, and salt and pepper and cover the pot. Cook for 12 to 15 minutes, until the burdock and parsnips are tender and can be easily pierced with a fork. Uncover the pot and cook for another 5 minutes so that the liquid reduces slightly. Use an immersion blender or transfer to a food processor and blend until the texture is similar to whipped cream. Let cool slightly and serve warm.

In January

Bitterroot Valley, Montana

Winter has been dragging its feet this year, which is fine by me, but the thought of getting hit hard with snow later this season tickles the back of my neck like a hardened murmur of dread.

What little snow is on the ground reflects the growing moon so well that it shines into my closed eyes, making sleep next to impossible. I unwillingly allow my thoughts to drift and my hand to reach for my phone every few minutes. There are watermelon radishes in the fridge that need to be pickled, a book to be written, and unanswered questions to the reality show I'm currently binging that must be googled. I'm feeling homesick yet completely enamored with my simple cabin life. Sleep escapes me, as it does most nights these days. I've struggled with insomnia for as long as I can remember, but it seems to be more enhanced the older I get. I'll go downstairs to remove myself from our tired bed and make myself something warm to drink.

Lavender Macaroons

Makes 15 macaroons

2 large egg whites, at room temperature

½ teaspoon salt

1 (14-ounce) bag shredded coconut flakes, unsweetened or sweetened

1 cup sweetened condensed milk

1 teaspoon dried lavender

1 teaspoon vanilla extract

Lavender macaroons were a bestseller at the farm's cafe in Sweden. They were made daily and consumed hastily by the customers. I mixed these up in large metal bowls in the kitchen and doled them out to the display case by the dozen. Not only are they simple to whip up but also they are great to make ahead and freeze for up to 2 months. Everyone loves a coconut macaroon, so these will always be a crowd pleaser. For extra fancieness, dip the macaroons in melted chocolate and let set before serving.

Preheat the oven to 350°F. Place the egg whites and salt in a large bowl and whisk using a hand mixer for 4 to 5 minutes, until stiff peaks have formed.

In a separate bowl, combine the coconut, sweetened condensed milk, lavender, and vanilla, then gently fold in the egg whites. Line a baking sheet with parchment paper. Using a small 1½ to 2-inch ice cream scoop, place the batter on the baking sheet, 2 to 3 inches apart. Bake the macaroons for 25 to 30 minutes, until the tops are a light golden brown color. Let cool before serving.

Everything Bagel and Herbs Seasoning

Makes about 2 cups

¼ cup sesame seeds

2 tablespoons
coarse sea salt

1 tablespoon
flaked kombu

¼ cup dried tulsi

2 tablespoons
dried nettle

¼ cup garlic flakes

¼ cup onion flakes

¼ cup poppy seeds

I'm definitely not the only person completely taken in by the everything bagel seasoning trend. It works for nearly everything: rice, soup, dips, actual bagels. . . . There's a reason that this seasoning has made its way into the hearts and cupboards of the people. I took this seasoning as a personal win as a New England bagel-loving person in the middle of Montana. It brought joy to my meals and still does. This is my herby take on this trendy little recipe. If your kombu flakes are too big for your shaker, give them a little mix in a blender or with mortar and pestle before adding to the mix.

Place all the ingredients in a large bowl and stir until well combined. Add more seasoning to taste. Keep in a pint-sized jar or shaker and store at room temperature for up to 1 month.

Creamy Tulsi and Sweet Pea Pasta

Serves 4

10 ounces spaghetti

1 cup green peas, shelled or frozen

½ cup unsalted butter or ghee

¼ cup all-purpose flour

½ cup heavy cream or milk

1 cup reserved pasta water

1 tablespoon tomato paste

2 to 4 tablespoons crushed garlic

1 tablespoon red pepper flakes

½ cup dried tulsi

1 teaspoon dried basil

Salt and freshly ground black pepper

I like making pasta dishes with dried herbs during colder months when I need something comforting, heavy, and uplifting, and this is the ultimate comfort food. Garlicky, creamy, and a little spicy, a pasta dish like this is a good essential to nail. Once you get the hang of making a roux, you'll be whipping them up left and right and impressing yourself and your friends. You can use whatever pasta you have handy. I'm a fan of twirling my pasta, so I used standard spaghetti, but it really is up to you and what you have on hand. Pair with Tulsi and Rosemary—Roasted Tomatoes with Peppered Mushrooms (page 114) or Roasted Asparagus with Chamomile and Ghee (page 66). You can also substitute garlic with 1 or 2 cloves of black garlic for a nice umami twist.

Begin by boiling heavily salted water. Place the pasta in the water and cook according to the package directions, making sure to reserve 1 cup of the pasta water before draining. If using frozen peas, I usually add them with the pasta as it cooks.

While the pasta is cooking, make your roux. Over medium heat, melt the butter in a medium saucepan. Once the butter has melted, add the flour 1 tablespoon at a time, whisking frequently. Once the butter and flour have formed into a thick paste, add the cream and continue to whisk frequently. This is key, as you don't want the roux to burn or get too clumpy.

Slowly add the reserved pasta water to the pan while whisking frequently. Once combined, turn the heat to low. Add the tomato paste, garlic, red pepper flakes, tulsi, and basil to the pan.

Combine well and add more pasta water or cream if the sauce is too thick. Drain the pasta and peas, then add them to the sauce. Season with salt and pepper to taste. Mix well and serve.

Nettle and Oysters Rockefeller

Makes 12 oysters

1 cup fresh spinach

¼ cup dried nettles

2 cloves garlic, minced

¼ cup chopped green onion

½ stick unsalted butter, melted

½ cup freshly grated Gruyère cheese

½ teaspoon red pepper flakes

¼ cup bread crumbs

1 teaspoon hot sauce

Salt and freshly ground black pepper

12 oysters, shucked and on the half shell

Fresh lemon wedges, for serving

Oysters are one of my all-time favorite things in the world. Not only do I love eating them but also I adore how they are grown and harvested. I have a collection of oysters shells from around the country that sit in a little terracotta pot on my staircase. Oysters Rockefeller makes me feel like I'm sitting in an old New York bar with a martini, covered in costume jewelry. They are classic and, without a doubt, damn delicious. Ask your local fish market whether they have larger oysters for baking. They're perfect for this dish and a little cheaper too!

Preheat the oven to 450°F. Place the spinach, nettles, garlic, green onions, and butter in a food processor. Pulse until the mix resembles pesto. Transfer to a large, clean bowl and add the Gruyère, red pepper flakes, bread crumbs, hot sauce, and salt and pepper. Mix until well combined.

Line a baking sheet with parchment paper. Lay the oysters on the baking sheet and add 1 tablespoon of the mixture on top of each oyster. Use up as much of the mix as you can. Bake the oysters for 8 minutes, until the cheese has browned. Serve warm with lemon wedges and eat with a fork.

Rosemary-Caramelized Onion Jam

Makes 1½ cups

3 large yellow onions, peeled, cut into ½-inch slices

¼ cup extra-virgin olive oil

½ cup balsamic vinegar

4 to 6 sprigs rosemary

1 cup cane sugar

Pinch of salt

Caramelized onions are possibly the perfect addition to most meals. This "jam" is a really nice way to jazz up a sandwich, pasta, or even just crackers and cheese (my personal favorite is chèvre). The first summer I spent in Sweden, my friend Jaclyn and I went through a phase of eating sautéed onions with a big chunk of goat cheese every day for lunch. I never got sick of it and could probably still eat that every day.

One thing about caramelizing onions is that you have to be patient— like, very patient. This recipe will take you about 1½ hours to make, but it is 100% worth it. Just remember to be patient, keep your heat low, and stir only occasionally! I've made this mistake a few times now, and it's always a disappointment. So again, be patient and trust the process!

✦ ✦ ✦

Place the oil in a large heavy-bottomed pan over low heat. Once hot, add the onions, making sure to coat them in the oil. Add the vinegar, rosemary, and sugar. Mix to coat the onions.

Cook the onions on low heat, stirring occasionally, for up to 1½ hours, or until the vinegar has reduced and become syrupy. Salt to your liking, then remove the pan from the heat and let the onions cool. Remove the larger rosemary sprigs, if desired.

Transfer the onions to an airtight container and keep them in the fridge for up to 2 weeks. Serve with meat or cheese or atop some roasted veggies.

Black Garlic Mashed Potatoes

Serves 4

1½ pounds fingerling potatoes, washed, skin on

2 cloves black garlic, peeled

½ cup unsalted butter

½ cup cream or milk, divided

Salt and freshly ground black pepper

As a kid, our family/friend meetup spot was a Canadian-themed restaurant near the Maine Mall called Bugaboo Creek. Aside from the thrill of their animatronic moose head that hung above the dining room and would occasionally address the guests, the best thing about that place was the mashed potatoes. Salty and made with the potato skins still on, the mashed potatoes were a must-have and quickly became a staple in our own household. Black garlic is one of my favorite ways to add a unique twist to a classic dish. A little goes a long way, and the flavor is umami enough that you won't need too many other seasonings. You kind of want the black garlic to take over and do its thing. I will, of course, smother my mashed potatoes in sriracha once they are on my plate. I can't help it.

+ + +

Place the potatoes in a large pot over medium-high heat. Cover them with water and bring to a boil. Once the water has begun to boil, decrease the heat to medium and continue cooking the potatoes until they're tender and can be easily punctured with a fork.

Remove the pot from the heat, drain the potatoes, and return them to the pot. Using a masher or fork, begin to mash the potatoes. Once the potatoes have started to break down, add the garlic, butter, and ¼ cup of the cream. Continue mashing, adding more cream to increase the smoothness. Season with salt and pepper to your liking. Once you've reached a desired consistency, serve warm.

Moon Milk

Serves 1

**1½ cups milk
of your choice**

**1 teaspoon ground
cinnamon**

**½ tablespoon
vanilla extract**

**1 heaping tablespoon
butterfly pea flowers**

**2 tablespoons Lavender
Simple Syrup (page 85)**

This is what I call Moon Milk. It's a lavendery version of the drink my grandparents used to make whenever I'd sleep over at their house as a child. To this day, warm milk with a little bit of vanilla and sugar hits the spot when I'm having trouble sleeping. You can use whatever sort of milk you like for this recipe. Use a handheld frother if you have one; otherwise, a simple whisk will do. Infuse a heaping spoon of butterfly pea flowers to turn it a lavender color. Butterfly pea flowers also come in a powdered version, which is easy to add to drinks. If using whole flowers, strain them out before serving.

Place the milk, cinnamon, vanilla, and butterfly pea flowers in a small pot and bring to a simmer over low heat, whisking frequently. Once warm, remove the pot from the heat and add the lavender syrup. Whisk or froth until well combined. Strain the mixture into a large mug and drink warm.

Pickled Onions

Makes 1½ cups

1 cup rice vinegar

1 cup champagne vinegar

1 tablespoon kosher salt

½ cup cane sugar

1 large red onion, skin removed, halved crosswise, cut into ½-inch slices

½ teaspoon black peppercorns

1 cinnamon stick

1 teaspoon crushed cardamom pods

Pickled onions are one of my go-to toppings. Nachos, salads, and even a big bowl of well-seasoned beans . . . you can't go wrong with pickled onions. I was initially intimidated by the process of pickling, but once I made these, I was hooked. Now the possibility for anything pickled is absolutely endless. When it comes to the herbs I use to season the onions, you can use whatever you have on hand—these are just my favorite. Bonus points if you have a few fresh dill flowers to toss in!

✦ ✦ ✦

Place the vinegars, salt, and sugar in a small pot over medium heat and bring to a simmer.

In a quart-sized jar, add the onions, peppercorns, cinnamon stick, and cardamom. Cover completely with the vinegar mixture and let cool before capping. The onions will be ready to consume within 24 hours. They will keep for up to 1 month in the fridge.

Chamomile Hot Toddy

Serves 1

1 high-quality
chamomile tea bag

1 ounce whiskey
or brandy

Lemon juice

Honey

1 cinnamon stick,
for garnish

This is something that is so beyond simple I'm almost astounded that I don't hear of it more often. I'm in no way a revolutionary when it comes to hot toddies, but this drink is often my go-to on cold nights when I can't sleep. Substitute whatever sleepy tea you have on hand, but chamomile is a favorite of mine and definitely encourages sleep and acts as a digestive aid.

Brew the tea according to the instructions on the package, leaving enough room in the mug for the ounce of whiskey. Add the whiskey and lemon juice to taste. Add the honey to your desired sweetness and stir well. Garnish with a cinnamon stick for extra flavor.

Acknowledgements

To the stewards of the Salish, Wampanoag, Pomo, and Wabanaki land, I want to acknowledge and extend my gratitude to you. I pay my respects to the elders past, present and emerging.

My husband and partner, Connor, life is easier with you in it. Thank you for bearing with me in every way possible, especially when it comes to my work. I love you more than I can even say.

My agent, Meg Thompson. If I could think of a million ways to thank you for your support, I would say them all every day. I'm so grateful our paths crossed and am always in awe of you.

Hilarie Burton, wow wow wow. Thank you for being such an inspiring new presence in my life. You do so much good in this world and I'm beyond thankful to know you.

My editor, Jean Lucas, thank you for advocating for this book to be made. I will always appreciate that. The rest of the Andrews McMeel team: Julie Barnes, Thea Voutiritsas, Elizabeth Garcia, Carol Coe, and Cat Vaughn, forever thankful.

Sierra McMurry, for taking some truly beautiful photos and becoming my friend in the process.

Summer Ashely, for listening to me word vomit about the book writing process, providing feedback, and always getting it.

My parents, for encouraging me to write and forge my own path regardless of how dismal it seemed at times. Glad to make it out on this side.

Leah Carlson-Stanisic, for taking the time to give me feedback on this cover. You are a true creative genius. (And I really mean it!)

Rachel D. Silver and Anja Rothe for taking the time to look over the book with your vast herbal wisdom.

Carol Artega, Jessica Lee Sabine, and Tori McCandless for providing some fun photos from our past.

Jill and Sophie, Robin Kerber, Dana Coughlin, Ash Molesso, Tasha Littlefield, Morgan Bowen, Ness Hutchins, Brittany Adelhardt, Zoe Haney, Maggie Smith, Asiah Mae, the Gibsons, the Mizners.

To everyone who has become my friend online or sent kind words via emails and DMs over the years.

Glossary of Herbal Actions

Herbal actions help identify the medicinal benefits of a plant. Each of the following actions can be found with a specific herb in the herbal pantry section (see page 17). When researching herbs, I love poring over books and matching the herbs to their actions. It feels oh so witchy and studious.

Adaptogen: Plants that help your body adapt to stress and build immunity. Adaptogens work best when used long term.

Analgesic: A substance used to reduce pain.

Antifungal: A plant used to prevent or treat fungal infections.

Anti-inflammatory: Herbs used to reduce inflammation.

Antispasmodic: An herb that relieves muscle spasms.

Antiviral: A substance used to prevent and ward off viruses.

Aphrodisiac: Foods, drinks, or herbs that arouse and stimulate sexual desire.

Aromatic: A plant containing volatile oils that release scents that stimulate, soothe, or please the spirit and mind.

Astringent: Herbs for drying, puckering, and drawing, either topically or internally, which help create a barrier for healing.

Bitter: Herbs that increase bile flow in the intestine, therefore aiding the process of digestion.

Carminative: Warming herbs that promote healthy digestion and ease bloating, constipation, and gas.

Demulcent: Herbs that produce a thick substance that protects mucous membranes, soothes irritation of the digestive tract, and decreases inflammation.

Diaphoretic: An herb that induces sweating.

Diuretic: Herbs that stimulate the elimination of fluid from the body.

Emmenagogue: Herbs that stimulate and increase menstrual flow.

Expectorant: An herb that helps break up and expel mucus in the lungs.

Nervine: Herbs that are soothing to the mind and calming to the nervous system.

Vulnerary: A plant used to aid the healing process of internal and external wounds.

Herbal resources

Bulk herbs

Mountain Rose Herbs
https://mountainroseherbs.com/

Frontier Co-op
https://www.frontiercoop.com/

Starwest Botanicals
https://www.starwest-botanicals.com/

My Go-To Herb Books:

Medical Herbalism, the Science and Practice of Herbal Medicine, David Hoffman (2003)

Herbal Recipes for Vibrant Health, Rosemary Gladstar (2003)
(really, any book by Rosemary Gladstar is going to be a good one to keep on your shelf)

The Herbal Medicine Maker's Handbook, James Green (2000)

The Book of Herbal Wisdom: Using Plants as Medicines, Matthew Wood (1997)

The Master Book of Herbalism, Paul Beyerl (1984)

Making Plant Medicine, Richo Cech (2000)

Education

Ancestral Apothecary
Online and Oakland, CA
https://ancestralapothecaryschool.com/

California School of Herbal Studies
Forestville, CA
https://cshs.com/

Chestnut School of Herbal Medicine
Online and Asheville, North Carolina
https://chestnutherbs.com/

RootWork Herbals
Online and Ithaca, New York
https://www.rootworkherbals.com/

Brands I Love

Herbal powders and other remedies:

Peak and Valley
https://peakandvalley.co/

Golde
https://golde.co/

Fat of the Land Apothecary
https://www.fatofthelandapothecary.com/

Avena Botanicals
https://www.avenabotanicals.com/

Other Loved Brands:

Fishwife Tinned Seafood Co.
https://eatfishwife.com/

Daybreak Seaweed Co.
https://daybreakseaweed.com/

West + Wilder Wine
(thoughtful canned wine for all
your forest adventures)
https://westandwilder.com/

The ill-fated dinner party

Metric Conversions and Equivalents

Approximate Metric Equivalents

Volume

¼ teaspoon	1 milliliter
½ teaspoon	2.5 milliliters
¾ teaspoon	4 milliliters
1 teaspoon	5 milliliters
1¼ teaspoon	6 milliliters
1½ teaspoon	7.5 milliliters
1¾ teaspoon	8.5 milliliters
2 teaspoons	10 milliliters
1 tablespoon (½ fluid ounce)	15 milliliters
2 tablespoons (1 fluid ounce)	30 milliliters
¼ cup	60 milliliters
⅓ cup	80 milliliters
½ cup (4 fluid ounces)	120 milliliters
⅔ cup	160 milliliters
¾ cup	180 milliliters
1 cup (8 fluid ounces)	240 milliliters
1¼ cups	300 milliliters
1½ cups (12 fluid ounces)	360 milliliters
1⅔ cups	400 milliliters
2 cups (1 pint)	480 milliliters
3 cups	720 milliliters
4 cups (1 quart)	0.96 liter
1 quart plus ¼ cup	1 liter
4 quarts (1 gallon)	3.8 liters

Weight

¼ ounce	7 grams
½ ounce	14 grams
¾ ounce	21 grams
1 ounce	28 grams
1¼ ounces	35 grams
1½ ounces	42.5 grams
1⅔ ounces	47 grams
2 ounces	57 grams
3 ounces	85 grams
4 ounces (¼ pound)	113 grams
5 ounces	142 grams
6 ounces	170 grams
7 ounces	198 grams
8 ounces (½ pound)	227 grams
16 ounces (1 pound)	454 grams
35.25 ounces (2.2 pounds)	1 kilogram

Length

⅛ inch	3 millimeters
¼ inch	6.25 millimeters
½ inch	1.25 centimeters
1 inch	2.5 centimeters
2 inches	5 centimeters
2½ inches	6.25 centimeters
4 inches	10 centimeters
5 inches	12.75 centimeters
6 inches	15.25 centimeters
12 inches (1 foot)	30.5 centimeters

Metric Conversion Formulas

To Convert	Multiply
Ounces to grams	Ounces by 28.35
Pounds to kilograms	Pounds by .454
Teaspoons to milliliters	Teaspoons by 4.93
Tablespoons to milliliters	Tablespoons by 14.79
Fluid ounces to milliliters	Fluid ounces by 29.57
Cups to milliliters	Cups by 240
Cups to liters	Cups by .236
Pints to liters	Pints by .473
Quarts to liters	Quarts by .946
Gallons to liters	Gallons by 3.785
Inches to centimeters	Inches by 2.54

Oven Temperatures

To convert Fahrenheit to Celsius, subtract 32 from Fahrenheit, multiply the result by 5, then divide by 9.

Description	Fahrenheit	Celsius	British Gas Mark
Very cool	200°	95°	0
Very cool	225°	110°	¼
Very cool	250°	120°	½
Cool	275°	135°	1
Cool	300°	150°	2
Warm	325°	165°	3
Moderate	350°	175°	4
Moderately hot	375°	190°	5
Fairly hot	400°	200°	6
Hot	425°	220°	7
Very hot	450°	230°	8
Very hot	475°	245°	9

Common Ingredients and Their Approximate Equivalents

1 cup uncooked white rice = 185 grams

1 cup all-purpose flour = 120 grams

1 stick butter (4 ounces • ½ cup • 8 tablespoons) = 110 grams

1 cup butter (8 ounces • 2 sticks • 16 tablespoons) = 220 grams

1 cup brown sugar, firmly packed = 213 grams

1 cup granulated sugar = 200 grams

Information compiled from a variety of sources, including *Recipes into Type* by Joan Whitman and Dolores Simon (Newton, MA: Biscuit Books, 1993); *The New Food Lover's Companion* by Sharon Tyler Herbst (Hauppauge, NY: Barron's, 2013); and *Rosemary Brown's Big Kitchen Instruction Book* (Kansas City, MO: Andrews McMeel, 1998).

Index

Forest +Home

Andrews McMeel Publishing
a division of Andrews McMeel Universal
1130 Walnut Street, Kansas City, Missouri 64106
www.andrewsmcmeel.com

22 23 24 25 26 SDB 10 9 8 7 6 5 4 3 2 1

ISBN: 978-1-5248-6765-2

Library of Congress Control Number: 2021952811

Editor: Jean Z. Lucas
Designer: Julie Barnes
Photographer: Spencre McGowan; Sierra McMurry: Pages vi, 21,
42, 72, 79, 117, 140; Connor Coughlin: Pages 130, 162, 192
Brand Manager: Cat Vaughn
Production Editors: Thea Voutiritsas and Elizabeth A. Garcia
Production Manager: Carol Coe

ATTENTION: SCHOOLS AND BUSINESSES

Andrews McMeel books are available at quantity discounts with
bulk purchase for educational, business, or sales promotional use.
For information, please e-mail the Andrews McMeel Publishing
Special Sales Department: specialsales@amuniversal.com.